# RAW DEAL

# RARE

## HORRIBLE AND IRONIC STORIES

BLAST BOOKS   NEW YORK

OF FORGOTTEN AMERICANS

ken smith

art by mack white

Blast Books gratefully acknowledges the generous help of Don Kennison.

Published by Blast Books, Inc.
P. O. Box 51, Cooper Station
New York, NY 10276-0051

ISBN 0-922233-20-9

DESIGNED BY LAURA LINDGREN

Typefaces in this book are Scala,
designed by Martin Majoor,
Bassuto, designed by Paul Hickson,
and Meta, designed by Erik Spiekermann.

Manufactured in the United States of America

First Edition 1998

10 9 8 7 6 5 4 3 2 1

*To be on the alert is to live,
to be lulled into security is to die.*
—OSCAR WILDE

# CONTENTS

# ACKNOWLEDGMENTS

Many thanks to the librarians and curators of the New York City public library system and the Center for the Humanities research center in Manhattan; the Newark and Harrison, New Jersey, public libraries; the Walsh Library at Seton Hall University, South Orange, New Jersey; the University of Miami Library, Coral Gables, Florida; the Pogue Library at Murray State University and the Wrather West Kentucky Museum, both of Murray, Kentucky; and the Menczer Museum of Medicine and Dentistry at the Hartford Medical Society, Hartford, Connecticut.

Thanks to family and friends, loyal and true; to librarian extraordinaire Jeanette Walker for research assistance; to Anne Bernstein and Henry Lowengard for helping find Mack White; to Mack White himself for his terrific art; and extra-special thanks to Dorian Devins for her insights, invaluable contributions, and kindness.

# A MESSAGE FROM KEN

Raw deals don't happen every day. For that we should be thankful. They happen to unusual people, or to average people thrust into horrible situations. Those qualities make for interesting stories, which is one of the reasons I wrote this book.

Another reason is that raw deals make me mad. Those who suffered them weren't only mistreated in life, they've been mistreated in death. Pariahs, oddballs, fish out of water, they had no fans to mourn their passing. Their pain served no purpose, taught no lessons. Before their stories were tossed into the dumpster of history, I felt they deserved one more chance to be told.

Raw deals are useful. Being extreme, they cast a harsh light on the dark side of human nature: ignorance, prejudice, fear, self-interest, hate. As you read about Ebenezer Cade or Sarah Winnemucca or Edwin Howard Armstrong, perhaps you'll recognize a similar raw deal lurking in your future. Then you can sidestep it before you become fodder for a future edition of this book.

There didn't seem to be any historian or scholar sufficiently superficial to cover the broad scope necessary for *Raw Deal*. Historians and scholars, to their credit, are masters of detail. *Raw Deal* needed someone who could find and evaluate the best available sources, decide what seemed appropriate, read, digest, and then write. For that, I considered myself qualified.

No grand plan governed who was and wasn't included in *Raw Deal*. Candidates only had to be in America and very, very unlucky. They also had to be dead at least twenty-five years—enough time, I reckoned, for those who destroyed them either to retire or die so that the nasty truths and appropriate documentation could float to the surface.

I've tried to keep the stories in *Raw Deal* brief by including only the facts I felt were necessary for a concise, accurate narrative. I apologize if this resulted in any disruptive omissions.

*Raw Deal* was written with a point of view, but I didn't consider that an excuse to be sloppy. To the best of my knowledge the facts presented here are correct. Any errors should be considered my own and should not reflect on the authors of my source material. For the opinions I've offered I am, of course, solely responsible.

*Raw Deal* would not exist without the researchers, journalists, and scholars who went before me and whose wealth of material I have humbly plundered. If the stories in *Raw Deal* interest you, I hope you'll visit your local library or book store and read the sources from which I gathered much of my material. They're listed in the select bibliography at the end of this book.

Since all the people featured in *Raw Deal* are dead, some might dismiss their stories as old and irrelevant. That would be a mistake. If you view the unpleasant fates suffered by the people in *Raw Deal* as historical abstractions, or if you believe that nothing of the sort could ever happen again, then you simply haven't been paying attention.

# 1

# Star of the
# Monkey House

NEW YORK CITY'S ZOOLOGICAL PARK HAD NEVER SEEN ANY-
thing like this. Forty thousand people poured through
its gates, an unheard-of total for a single day in the off-
season even for the largest zoo on earth. Families came.
So did fashionable young women and men. Most important for the bottom line, so did the huddled masses usually drawn to less-refined entertainment.

Zoological Park was uptown, in the Bronx. It tradition-
ally courted the well-heeled and enlightened for afternoons
of gentle amusement. Not anymore—now that the zoo had
an attraction not even brash Coney Island could match.

His name was Ota Benga. If nothing else, he was hon-
estly billed: a genuine African pygmy and a possible one-
time eater of human flesh. He was, in the opinion of those
who put him in the Monkey House, a very lucky pygmy.

How he got into a cage in New York City is an odd story. It took over two years of intercontinental travel, a hiatus at a world's fair, and the combined efforts of a bankrupt Presbyterian missionary and a man who believed that the highest honor achievable by an animal was to be exhibited in a zoo.

Ota was a member of the Chirichiri people and had lived in the forests of equatorial Africa near the Kasai River. His first wife had been captured by a neighboring tribe and, reportedly, eaten. His second had stepped on the head of a viper and died of snakebite. Ota, however, was healthy, young, and eager; those who knew him called him "Bi," which simply meant "friend." His most distinguishing physical feature—other than his short-ness—was his teeth, which he had filed into daggerlike points.

Six thousand miles from Ota Benga's home, visionaries and architects in St. Louis, Missouri, were planning a world's fair. In their minds, the St. Louis Louisiana Purchase Exposition of 1904 would be unlike any fair that had gone before. It would have a serious, almost cerebral underpinning. It would show its visitors not only where they were headed, but where they had come from.

Exposition planners created an anthropology department to showcase the history of human development. It hired special agents to comb the earth gathering exhibits. One of these was the Reverend Samuel Phillips Verner, a Presbyterian missionary and professor at Stillman Institute, a college for blacks in Tuscaloosa, Alabama. His mission: recruit tribal Africans to populate a replica pygmy village. His written orders from the anthropology department were clear: "Get the pygmies."

Verner met Ota Benga in March 1904, when Ota was a captive in the slave market of the Baschiele tribe. The Belgian army, which was subjugating the region at the time, brought Ota to Verner's attention and mentioned that the Baschiele sometimes ate their captives. Verner bought Ota for five dollars' worth of provisions, then offered him the chance to come to America. Ota wasn't sure; he thought Verner had come from the Land of the Dead and practiced witchcraft. Still, it might be better than being a slave and possibly eaten. Sensing little opportunity at home, Ota agreed.

The next day Verner wrote to Dr. W. J. McGee, chief of the anthropology department, "The first pygmy has been secured!"

After he had struck a deal with Ota, Verner recruited eight other Africans to complete the pygmy village. By the first of July, the pygmies were in St. Louis and on display. It wasn't much of a community; there were no women, and the pygmies were housed in a tent behind a fence. They had to borrow blankets from their neighbors in the American Indian building to keep warm.

This was no carnival sideshow, the *New York Times* reported. "Extensive sets of measurements are to be taken, and tests made of all the tribes available, and it is expected that important data will be collected to serve as the basis of subsequent anthropological study." Other human exhibits showcased at the fair included Eskimos from Greenland, Ainus from Japan, and Patagonians from South America.

Ota was a favorite with the public. He never admitted cannibalism, but his dagger teeth raised dark possibilities in the minds of fairgoers (none of the other pygmies had them). He would open his mouth and grin for a nickel. The people of St. Louis, finding Ota's name hard to pronounce, called him "Autobank."

The pygmies lived at the exposition for six months. When the fair closed in December, each was given a fifty-cent pocket watch chain and fifteen cents in spending money. With Verner again in the lead, they then took a ship back to the Kasai. Eight of them returned to their homes and vanished from American history.

Ota did not. When he and Verner arrived at his village, Ota discovered that the last of his relatives were dead. He also found that his tribal chief was dying, and he suspected that certain individuals would be eaten to soothe the spirits of the dead. Ota was convinced he would be one of the chosen victims. He decided, once again, to go to America.

Ota's whereabouts over the following eighteen months are hazy. Apparently Verner left his teaching position and supported himself by giving lectures. Ota was probably used as an audio-visual aid.

Back in New York, Director William T. Hornaday was running New York Zoological Park the way he saw fit. He was a man with a flair for showmanship, always on the lookout for "something new under the sun" to draw a crowd—particularly after the summer season.

The ultimate exhibit for any zoo, he believed, was another human being. He wanted to make this happen in New York by building a replica Indian village where the original "noble aborigines of Manhattan" would live and be on display—like his other honored animals. It was a dream that was never realized, probably because by 1906 all members of New York's aboriginal tribes were either dead or not in the mood to participate in Director Hornaday's grand scheme.

Still, the idea was out there. In 1897 Robert Peary brought six live Eskimos back from his polar expedition and lent them to New York's Museum of Natural History. Four of them promptly died; the museum dissected them and added their bones to its collection. The 1904 St. Louis Exposition proved the workability of the concept on a grand scale. It was only a matter of time before Hornaday would get his chance.

Opportunity literally knocked on the director's door in early September 1906, when Verner showed up with a chimpanzee and Ota. Verner needed cash while he looked for a job in Manhattan and was willing to sell the chimp for $275. Hornaday eyed Ota. The pygmy was not a Manhattan native, but he was aboriginal.

The zoo would be happy to buy the chimp, Hornaday replied. By the way, since Verner was tied up in a job search, why not leave Ota at the zoo as well? Hornaday promised to pay for Ota's keep and give him a good home for as long as Verner needed to pound the pavement. In exchange, the zoo would use Ota as turnstile bait. Verner thought it a reasonable idea. He and Hornaday agreed that the best place for Ota was in the Monkey House.

The next day—Saturday, September 8—Ota was given a supply of straw to weave a hammock and was introduced to his new home. The Monkey House had a large, open-air compound where the chimps and Dohong, an orang-utan, gave performances. Individual cages opened onto this enclosed courtyard. Ota hung his hammock in the empty cage next to Dohong's. The keepers put a target in the enclosure; Ota was given a bow and arrows and encouraged to come out of his cage and shoot.

Director Hornaday ordered bones scattered around the floor of the compound to add atmosphere. He also had an informative sign hung outside Ota's cage, listing his height (4' 11") and weight (103 lbs.) and noting that he would be "exhibited each afternoon during September."

To Hornaday's delight, word got around fast. Ota was an immediate sensation. The *New York Times* ran an article: BUSHMAN SHARES A CAGE WITH BRONX PARK APES. Thousands of curious New Yorkers made the long trek uptown to the zoo. "Where's the wild man?" they all asked at the gate.

Dohong, who in earlier days had to peddle a bicycle to entertain visitors, now was allowed inside the main enclosure to romp with Ota. When Ota wasn't at target practice or wrestling with the orangutan, the zookeepers encouraged him to charge the bars of his cage, teeth bared, to give children a scare. The crowds roared with laughter at everything he did. Nearly everyone appeared happy with the arrangement. Everyone, that is, except the clergy of New York's black Baptist churches.

Led by James H. Gordon, superintendent of the Howard Colored Orphan Asylum in Brooklyn, the clergy opposed the Monkey House show on fundamentalist religious grounds, noting, "The exhibition evidently aims to be a demonstration of the Darwinist theory of evolution." They also opposed it on ethical principle. "Our race, we think, is depressed enough," Gordon said, "without exhibiting one of us with the apes."

Gordon and the clergy demanded a meeting with New York mayor George McClellan. He agreed, then let them cool their heels in a city hall anteroom, then dismissed them with a note explaining he was too busy. He suggested they take their complaints to the New York Zoological Society.

Meanwhile, the local press was beginning to ask Director Hornaday to explain the rationale behind his new attraction. He defended Ota Benga's presence on the grounds of practicality and public service. "As for the boy being exhibited in the cage," he told the *New York Globe,* "it was done simply for the convenience of the thousands of people who wanted to see him." He added, proudly, "He has one of the best rooms in the primate house."

Nevertheless, Hornaday decided to modify Ota's presentation. The staged shows of Ota and Dohong romping in the compound ended, though Ota could still be found amusing the crowds in the Monkey House when he wasn't roaming the grounds. This was the new twist. Ota was allowed to wander freely, though a keeper was always close at hand. Crowds followed him. Some poked him in the ribs. Others tripped him. Everyone laughed.

This might have gone on indefinitely, but Ota quickly grew weary of the attention. His newfound mobility offered no relief, but it did give him access to the director's office. Ota decided to express his displeasure by hanging his hammock over Hornaday's desk, crawling into it, and tormenting the director with blasts from a harmonica. He did not appreciate being one of Hornaday's honored animals. Hornaday could do nothing to punish Ota; he was already under too much public scrutiny. And he couldn't release Ota until he had Verner's permission.

Verner, meanwhile, was nowhere to be found. He had gone to North Carolina and was apparently in no hurry to return—not until Hornaday paid him the balance of his $275.

Before long, Ota caused a fuss by shooting one of his obnoxious pursuers with an arrow. It got worse on September 25, when Ota slashed at his keepers with a knife when they tried to stop him from stripping in public (it was a hot day). Ota was overpowered and driven into his cage.

That was enough for Director Hornaday. Verner came to New York in the last week of September and was paid his money. On September 28, Ota was released from the zoo and taken to the Howard Colored Orphan Asylum, much to the relief of New York's black Baptist clergy and William T. Hornaday. Ota presented his bow and arrows to his keepers as souvenirs.

A few days later, the *New York Times* published a letter from a sixty-seven-year-old Parisian woman who wanted to know if Ota was "in good condition" and if the zoo would sell him to her "not too dear as I am not rich." The *Times* and Director Hornaday declined response.

Ota dropped out of the public's imagination as quickly as he had captured it. It had all been grand fun, but the people of New York could move on to other diversions. Ota could not. Now he was completely alone. The nearest member of his tribe was six thousand miles away. Verner, the closest thing he had to a friend, was broke and working night shifts as a ticket taker for the New York City subway.

At the asylum, Ota was given a suit of clothes and a room where he could smoke. He was taught English to replace his native "monkey language" and was pressured to convert to Christianity. The Baptists put caps on his filed teeth. Verner protested, insisting that the best thing for Ota would be to return to Africa. But neither Verner nor Ota had the cash to get him there, and Ota wasn't sure he wanted to go. He still feared that his tribe would eat him.

Four years after his zoo appearance, Ota was sent to the Virginia Theological Seminary and College, an all-black school in Lynchburg, Virginia. He would remain in Lynchburg the rest of his life. War between Africa's white landlords had broken up the kingdoms where Ota had lived. Now he couldn't return even if he wanted to.

Ota quit school and took a job in a tobacco factory, where his fellow workers called him "Bingo." He would tell the story of his life for root beer and sandwiches.

On March 20, 1916, Ota Benga built a fire outside the carriage house where he slept. He stripped to his loin cloth and broke the caps off his teeth. He retrieved a stolen revolver he had hidden under some hay, put the gun to his heart, and fired. He was only thirty-two. The city of Lynchburg buried him in an unmarked grave.

The *New York Times* asked Sam Verner to comment. "Between the impossible conditions of Ota Benga's own land and those which he could not surmount in ours," he replied, "can we wonder that he gave up his little life as an unsolvable problem?"

The *Lynchburg News* asked the same question of William Hornaday. "Evidently," Hornaday replied, "he felt that he would rather die than work for a living."

# 2

# The Perfect Instrument

CAN A PERSON BE DESTROYED BY A NOBLE VISION? BEFORE you answer, consider the story of Thaddeus Cahill and his remarkable creation, the Telharmonium.

Thaddeus was born in Iowa in 1867, the eldest son of a Harvard-trained physician. His father sensed that the boy was destined for greatness and tutored him at home. By the time Thaddeus reached his mid-twenties, he had graduated at the top of his law-school class and had a job as a congressional aid in Washington. His future seemed if not exceptional, full of promise.

But Thaddeus also had a dream. He wanted to build the perfect musical instrument.

In Thaddeus's time, music could be heard only by live performance or in Gramophone recordings. The live music heard by most people was performed by poorly trained local musicians on what Thaddeus considered imperfect instruments. Gramophone reproduction was thin and scratchy. With these limited options, only the wealthy and privileged could enjoy orchestral music that sounded good.

Thaddeus wanted to change this. He could do nothing about mediocre performers. But he could do something about mediocre instruments. He reasoned that if everyone had access to an instrument that could perfectly reproduce the sounds made by every other instrument, they would at last have a chance to hear perfect music.

Thaddeus began to study and then he began to tinker. He decided that the way to produce perfect music was to abandon wood and brass and individual craftsmanship. Instead, Thaddeus's new instrument—later christened the Telharmonium—would use iron and steel and machine-tool precision. There would be no rasp of a bow against string, no jarring slam of piano hammers into wires that had gone out of tune. In the Telharmonium, every conceivable note would be permanently frozen into toothed gearing and set free by electricity. The machine would then blend these mathematically precise sounds, duplicating an entire orchestra by itself.

It was a big project, but Thaddeus wasn't afraid to think big. By 1900, he had marshaled the time and energy to build an experimental model. Measured by the standards of its successors, it was small. It weighed only seven tons.

The first Telharmonium proved to Thaddeus that his theories were correct. He immediately began work on a commercial model, infinitely more complex than the first. Thaddeus quit his Washington job and moved to a machine shop in Massachusetts to supervise construction. Spirited, unflagging, sure of purpose, he labored seven days a week. Assisting him, sharing his vision, were his two brothers and two of his sisters. Three of the four, like Thaddeus, would never marry. All would devote their entire adult lives to the ideal of perfect music for everyone.

Thaddeus's vision quickly ran into a wall of technology. A turn-of-the-twentieth-century machine that could do everything that Thaddeus demanded required hundreds of alternators, transformers, tone mixers, rheostats, and induction coils, as well as thousands of relays and miles of wiring. The equipment for this new Telharmonium would eventually fill two railway boxcars. Obviously, it would be impossible to put one in somebody's parlor.

A man of less passion would have tried to adapt. Perhaps he would have designed a smaller machine with fewer capabilities. Not Thaddeus Cahill. Fewer capabilities meant imperfection, and Thaddeus would have none of that. The commercial Telharmonium had to remain as it was—all four hundred thousand pounds of it.

Thaddeus decided that the way to bring his perfect music to the people was by broadcasting—a bold idea for the time. Radio was in its infancy and it was noisy; static would corrupt the perfect sounds that Thaddeus was working so hard to create. Thaddeus decided, instead, to use the telephone.

The Telharmonium's electric music could be fed directly into a phone line and distributed with no loss of fidelity, no distortion, and no noise. But without amplifiers or loudspeakers, which hadn't yet been invented, how could a Telharmonium signal emerge from a telephone receiver, possibly hundreds of miles away, and fill a room with music? Thaddeus knew the answer: massive power. Juice the Telharmonium with several thousand volts, and its distortion-proof sound would erupt from any receiver, anywhere, clear and strong.

Thaddeus had solved the problem of imperfect music and, through broadcasting, the problem of imperfect musicians as well. With just a handful of mighty Telharmoniums providing music for the entire world, only the best performers would keep their jobs. All a person had to do was flick a switch, and the sweetest music ever manufactured would flow from the telephone.

With all technical issues resolved to Thaddeus's satisfaction, the first commercial Telharmonium was pressed into service. Development companies sold stock and built the lavish Telharmonic Hall in the heart of Manhattan's theater district. In early 1907 daily Telharmonium concerts were offered to the paying public. Special Telharmony telephone lines were run to fashionable restaurants and hotels where well-heeled customers could hear the wonders of "music on tap." Investors were courted, the press was wooed, capital began to flow in.

Honored guests were taken to the basement of Telharmonic Hall, where they would shake their heads in wonder as they witnessed the instrument in action. Eight "pitch shafts," each almost a foot wide and twenty yards long, rested on a mainframe of steel beams that covered a half acre. Mounted along them were hundreds of huge multiple-alternator steel rotors and dynamos, which when spinning produced the necessary notes and harmonics—a seven-octave range for each shaft. Gears linked the pitch shafts to one another, ensuring that the machine would remain forever in tune with itself. Exposed wires and cables cascaded down from the ceiling; nearly two thousand switches filled ten separate panels. Watching the guts of the Telharmonium in concert was like visiting a power plant: junctions chattered, sparks popped, generators whirred, transformers hummed. Only the audience above heard music.

The performance console of the Telharmonium was just as intimidating. It had eight banks of 672 keys and it took two musicians to play it. The first used four banks to play the melody, which required strong hands and a long reach to depress keys simultaneously that were often several banks apart. The second played the accompaniment on the remaining 336 keys—and adjusted the 200 knife switches that varied the volume of each harmonic and the attack and sustain of each chord; operated the four foot pedals that produced swell; manipulated yet another bank of 67 keys that produced rapid volume changes; and adjusted the master tuning rheostat if the pitch began to drift.

In the beginning, the public applauded this new sensation. The press dubbed the instrument "the many-mouthed musical giant" and called its concerts "The Music of A.D. 2000." People were both delighted and mystified to hear clear, pretty tunes emerge from ordinary telephone receivers and fill a room. The reproduction of the various instruments, while still not perfect, was close enough.

Investors, with an eye toward profit, eagerly scanned the potential markets listed in the Telharmonium prospectus. An estimated fifteen to twenty thousand receivers could be served by a single instrument. Theaters, stores, churches, schools, hospitals—even outdoor parks and amusement piers—all would pay handsomely to "rent music." Four separate channels were planned: ragtime, dance, classical, and sacred. A fifth channel would provide music on request. Thaddeus even envisioned a special "sleep-music" channel for home use.

The Telharmonium seemed still more marvelous when it was discovered that its music could be broadcast through the carbon arc lights used in factories and streetlamps. Company promoters boasted that the "Singing Arc Light" was only the beginning; with electrical vibration Thaddeus Cahill could "get music out of almost anything." There would be no end to the money-making possibilities of the Telharmonium.

Thaddeus Cahill's years of hard labor and bulldog tenacity—and his refusal to compromise his principles—had finally paid off. He returned to Massachusetts in triumph to begin work on a new, even mightier Telharmonium. The prize of perfect music for everyone seemed within reach.

The end of the Telharmonium was abrupt. Thaddeus's acceptance of it took years.

The first blow came in late 1907 when the stock market crashed, followed by a deep business depression. With thousands of companies bankrupt and tens of thousands of workers unemployed, investor capital dried up—particularly for unconventional ventures like the Telharmonium.

The second blow was even more devastating. The New York Telephone Company threw the Telharmonium off its phone lines.

Telharmonium and telephone wires ran side by side. Since Telharmonium signals were sometimes millions of times stronger than telephone signals—thanks to Thaddeus's need for amplifying power—they easily bled into the phone lines. People began to complain that Beethoven was muscling into their conversations. The New York Telephone Company, already defending itself against charges of poor service and shoddy business practices, didn't need another headache. Telharmonium service was shut off.

Still, there were the concerts in Telharmonic Hall. The company might survive on this income until it could run its own transmission lines—if it could keep up attendance. But the novelty of hearing pretty music from a phone receiver had passed. Attendance dwindled. Anxious Telharmonium backers, searching for new angles, turned Telharmonic Hall into a musical freak show. Classical compositions were cut and a bagpipe simulation was added. The Singing Arc Light became the principal attraction, as well as music broadcast from lily pads, doorknobs, and a hydrangea bush. At one point in each show a Telharmonium transmission wire was strapped to a member of the audience, turning that person into a Telharmonium receiver.

It didn't help. In mid-February 1908, Telharmonic Hall closed its doors for good. By summer, the last of the Telharmonium development companies had gone belly-up as well.

Thaddeus Cahill did not falter. If New York audiences didn't want perfect music, there were millions of people who did. If New York investors didn't want to back Thaddeus's dream, the Cahills would pay for it themselves.

Thaddeus and his siblings sank $300,000 of their own money—everything they had—into the third Telharmonium. It had improved alternators, more pitch shafts, smaller switchboards, and a simplified performance console. It was the most expensive musical instrument ever built.

The press, the investors, the *people*—ignored it.

This last blow was the hardest to accept. Its implications were inescapable: people didn't want perfect music. They didn't care about pure intonation and flawless harmonics. While Thaddeus had been locked in his New England machine shop, popular tastes had changed. People in 1914 would rather fox trot to *Ballin' the Jack* than sit and listen to Grieg's *Det Förste Möde,* no matter how flawlessly it was played.

The technology on everybody's lips was no longer the Telharmonium—it was radio. Radio, the upstart that Thaddeus and his partners had dismissed. Even though it was noisy it could carry all kinds of music—and the human voice as well.

Thaddeus and his brothers moved the third Telharmonium to Manhattan and gave private recitals. For eight years they pitched and pleaded. Thaddeus explained to anyone who would listen that this new machine would cost less per year to operate than a hundred-piece union-rate orchestra. He even changed its name to "Dynamo-phone" and then "Electrophone" to avoid raising memories of failed past projects.

No one was interested.

Seven companies had been formed over the course of a dozen years to fund the development of the Telharmonium. They poured an estimated $2 million into the project, an immense sum for the time. All of it had been lost. The two commercial Telharmoniums were broken up and sold for scrap. Thaddeus lived until 1934—forced to hear tinny, imperfect music on the radio—and then died of a heart attack.

Little remained of Thaddeus's dream—only the patent applications, a few enigmatic photographs, and some contemporary descriptions. No recordings were ever made of Telharmonium music. Thaddeus apparently felt that the raspy reproductions of the time would do injustice to his perfect creation.

Thaddeus's youngest brother, Arthur, the last surviving Cahill, kept the original seven-ton Telharmonium in the family garage. Its belts had rotted, its wires decayed, its meticulously lathed steel rotors rusted into inoperability. Still, it was the last remnant of Thaddeus's work. Arthur wrote to several museums in the hope that someone would preserve "this priceless monument to man's genius." No one accepted the offer.

In 1958, at age eighty-seven, Arthur finally sold the house and moved into an apartment. The great machine was left behind. The last Telharmonium, along with a box containing Thaddeus Cahill's ashes, was thrown away.

# Bummer

Frank Olson was a family man. He lived with his wife, Alice, and their three young children in the town of Frederick, Maryland, a postcard-perfect community nestled in the foothills of the Appalachian Mountains. Although he spent most of his free time at home, he was still considered outgoing and popular by his co-workers, who shared his good-natured practical jokes. Judging by the number of people who would attend his funeral, he had a lot of friends.

Unknown to most of them and even to his family, Frank Olson was neck deep in some of the dirtiest business in America. He worked as a civilian biochemist for the Special Operations Division (SOD) of the Army Chemical Corps. His specialty was bacteriological warfare, focusing on the airborne distribution of biological germs. Other chemists at the SOD would develop virulent strains of deadly diseases, such as botulism and anthrax, and Frank Olson would figure out how to get them into mundane-looking containers. "Antipersonnel harassment and assassination delivery systems," the army called them. Favorite delivery systems included underarm deodorants, shaving cream, and bug sprays. Olson had been at it for ten years and he was good.

Frank Olson labored for the SOD from 1943 to 1953, from World War II to the Korean War and during all the Cold War years between. It was a dark, suspicious decade, when Hitler, Stalin, and Joseph McCarthy cast long shadows. If Olson harbored any doubts about his work—and it later appeared that he harbored quiet a few—he conformed to the cautious tenor of the times and kept them to himself.

While Olson was busying himself with germ weapons for the army, a man named Sid Gottlieb was investigating drug weapons for the CIA. Sid Gottlieb's team, code named MK-Ultra, was one of dozens within both the agency and the military intelligence services that were studying—and using—narcotics as tools of espionage, tactical warfare, and political chaos. Their experiments covered the entire pharmacopoeia, from mescaline to hashish to cocaine to heroin. One team even produced a syrupy liquid marijuana, which they injected into cigarettes and used as a "truth drug." Future projects would not be as benign. Proposals ranged from pills that killed instantly to mass poisonings of city water supplies to drugs that could induce cancer, a stroke, or a heart attack without leaving a trace. Gottlieb's considerable energies were focused on LSD and the reactions it would produce when given to an unsuspecting human being.

LSD fascinated the spooks at MK-Ultra. It was colorless, odorless, and tasteless, and it was so powerful that it could send a man into another world with an amount no bigger than the "e" at the end of this sentence. Its effects were too unpredictable to make it useful as either an interrogation or brainwashing drug. Still, it was unacceptable to Gottlieb that such a potent hallucinogen would have no use as a weapon. He had only to keep trying it out on people, and he would eventually discover its useful—that is, vicious—side.

Finding the right people was a problem. For months the MK-Ultra team had been testing LSD on themselves, tripping in their offices and at agency parties, sometimes spiking each other's food without warning. In the outside world, MK-Ultra bankrolled researchers at the universities of Oklahoma, Illinois, and Rochester, New York, who tested LSD on student volunteers. MK-Ultra paid the doctors at the Addiction Research Center in Lexington, Kentucky, supposedly a rehabilitation facility for convicted addicts, to give prisoners LSD and record their reactions. One group of seven men was kept tripping on LSD for a mind-boggling seventy-seven consecutive days. Yet Gottlieb wasn't satisfied. All of these people were willing participants; most knew they were ingesting a drug and those who didn't, like the MK-Ultra men, were well aware of its effects. Gottlieb needed to know how unwilling, inexperienced, "normal" people would react. After all, those were the people that the CIA wanted to mess up with LSD.

Gottlieb's bosses forbade him to give LSD to unsuspecting outsiders without authorization, but Gottlieb was eager and thought he saw a clever way around the ban. The biannual three-day brainstorming retreat between MK-Ultra and the men of SOD—Frank Olson's group—was near. The SOD chemists were similar in spirit to Gottlieb's team. They knew, and accepted, the hazards of working with chemicals as weapons, but they had no experience with hallucinogenic drugs. It wasn't a perfect fit, but to Gottlieb it seemed a pretty good match of need to availability.

The first two days of the retreat passed uneventfully. The location was perfect for a meeting of spies: an isolated place called Deep Creek Lodge, built years earlier by the Boy Scouts deep in the woods of western Maryland. The principal topic of discussion was MK-Naomi, a joint project between the two teams that had the SOD building germ weapons for the CIA. Frank Olson described some of his newest products: a cigarette lighter that emitted lethal gas, lipstick that would kill on contact, a pocket spray for asthmatics that actually induced pneumonia. The CIA operatives were delighted.

Sid Gottlieb later insisted that he mentioned MK-Ultra's planned testing of LSD on unsuspecting outsiders to the men at Deep Creek Lodge. According to Gottlieb, everyone agreed that such experiments were necessary and that they would provide valuable information. When questioned later, no one besides Gottlieb remembered any such thing. Even if such a vague discussion had occurred, it didn't qualify as anything near informed consent. But for Gottlieb, anxious to get things rolling, it was close enough.

Thursday evening, November 19, 1953: the conferees gathered around the fireplace as Gottlieb poured after-dinner drinks for Olson, himself, and six others. A chummy cocktail among professional equals. After about twenty minutes of conversation, Gottlieb sprang the news. He had spiked the drinks with LSD.

Those who've taken acid know the importance of the "set" and the "setting"; both should be positive and non-threatening to help ensure a gentle psychoactive experience. Frank Olson, in contrast, had the set of a secretly worried, self-doubting man. And his setting—a remote cabin, surrounded by gleeful spooks who had tricked him into becoming a mind-control guinea pig—was not one conducive to trusting thoughts.

Within an hour, Olson began to behave strangely. His emotions bounced between pointless laughter, anger, and weeping. He couldn't understand what was happening to him. Over and over he claimed that someone was playing tricks with his mind and that there was a conspiracy to embarrass and ruin him. He became anxious, then depressed, then paranoid.

Sid Gottlieb and his team were puzzled. Bad trips were fairly common among the pathologically suspicious MK-Ultra men, but nothing like this had ever happened before. Certainly no student volunteer or drug-hardened convict had ever sunk into such a deep funk. Then again, they hadn't been duped into ingesting an extremely powerful hallucinogen, and they didn't make germ-warfare weapons for a living.

By Friday morning the dazed and groggy LSD trippers, even the unsuspecting ones, had come down and returned to the real world. Not Frank Olson. He was still despondent and disturbed. A CIA report later branded his actions "clear signs of psychotic behavior." Gottlieb, lacking a better alternative, sent Olson home to his wife.

Alice Olson was stunned by her husband's haggard appearance when he straggled home. His emotional state was even worse than his physical condition. He refused to tell her anything of what had happened. In fact, he refused to say anything, period. After much coaxing from Alice, Frank finally confessed that he had made "a terrible mistake" and that his colleagues had laughed at him. He would tell her nothing more.

This was very odd behavior for Frank Olson, who had always been at least cheerful in his secrecy. The practical jokester, the gregarious family man, had vanished. (The CIA later claimed that Frank Olson had "a suicidal tendency" for five years, a charge that Alice Olson vehemently denied.) His depression only grew worse as the weekend progressed.

The LSD was long gone from Frank Olson's system, but its powerful effects had snapped a vital brace in his mind. The mistrust and uncertainties he had hidden were now out in the open. With his schizoid life, to whom could he turn? Everything he did, everything that *mattered* was top secret. The only people he could talk to were the people he feared.

The first thing Monday morning, Frank Olson paid a visit to his boss at the SOD. Olson offered to quit or be fired. His boss, stunned and unaware of Gottlieb's shenanigans, reassured Olson that everything was fine with his work. But the next day found Olson even more disturbed. He complained of being "all mixed up" and insisted that he was incompetent. His boss, now aware that the CIA retreat had something to do with his biochemist's odd behavior, called Gottlieb's deputy, Robert Lashbrook, and urged him to send Olson to a psychiatrist.

This was a critical moment. Olson was already seriously unbalanced, but with proper counseling and the support of his family he might have pulled through. Lashbrook, however, did not call a psychiatrist. Instead, he called Sid Gottlieb. The two men, fearful that their careers would suffer if their disobedience was discovered, decided it was best to pack Frank Olson off to Manhattan to see a man named Harold Abramson.

Abramson wasn't a psychiatrist, a psychologist, or a psychotherapist. He was chief of the allergy clinic at New York's Mount Sinai Hospital. He was also one of the agency's most enthusiastic LSD contractors. Gottlieb knew he could be counted on to keep Olson quiet. This man, to whom Frank Olson's fragile psyche was now entrusted, had originally come to Gottlieb's attention with a proposal to give unknowing, mentally sound Mount Sinai patients LSD for "psychotherapeutic purposes." Gottlieb liked that attitude and had MK-Ultra bankroll Abramson's hospital research, where he was ordered to study LSD's potential to twist sex patterns, create embarrassing behavior, and addict its users.

By the time Olson arrived in Abramson's office, his personality was shattered. He seemed unaware of his own identity, repeatedly examining parts of his body as if they didn't belong to him. His feelings of depression, inadequacy, guilt, and suspicion had deepened. He told Abramson that the CIA was out to get him; that agents were putting Benzedrine in his coffee to keep him awake. Abramson's solution was to put Olson to bed with a glass of bourbon and some Nembutal ("yellow jackets"). It didn't help.

The next day, Abramson tried to cheer up Olson by sending him to see a magician who was on the CIA payroll. The magician, oblivious to Olson's condition, showed him how sleight of hand could be used to slip drugs into unsuspecting people's drinks. This was not the kind of thing that Olson needed to see. Instead of being entertained, he became paranoid. He believed that the magician would make him vanish.

Abramson gave Olson permission to return home the next day, Thanksgiving, to be with his family. That evening Olson's anxious behavior and delusions of persecution grew worse. He said that people were plotting against him and that he heard threatening voices. Lashbrook took Olson to a Broadway show, but Olson quickly became frightened; he knew that people were waiting outside to arrest him. Later that night, Olson snuck out of his hotel room and wandered the streets. Convinced that he was on a secret mission, listening to the voices that told him he had to erase his identity, he tore up all the money in his wallet, scattered the scraps in the subway, then threw the billfold away. Lashbrook found him in the hotel lobby at 5:30 the next morning, his hat and coat still on.

Olson was flown back to Washington as planned but he got little farther. On the ride out to Frederick he told Lashbrook to turn back. He didn't want to go home, he pleaded. He was "ashamed" and afraid he "would do something wrong in front of the children." Lashbrook dutifully took Olson back to the airport, then back to Manhattan.

By now, even the ever-optimistic Abramson recognized that Olson was a seriously sick man who needed hospitalization. He called Gottlieb, and the two agreed to send Olson to Chestnut Lodge, a sanitarium near Rockville, Maryland, staffed with CIA-cleared psychiatrists. It would mean that Gottlieb's secret test would be revealed to his superiors, but he couldn't keep Olson hidden any longer. Olson was allowed to call Alice and talk to her for the first time since he'd left for work on Tuesday morning, three days earlier. He told her that he felt much better. "Everything is going to be fine," he said.

That night Lashbrook shared a room with Olson at the Statler Hotel. In the early hours of Saturday morning, November 28, 1953, Lashbrook awoke just in time to see the dark shape of Olson dashing across the room. Olson hit the window at full speed, crashing through it and screaming as he plunged to the sidewalk ten stories below. By the time the thud of his impact reached Lashbrook, Frank Olson was dead.

Clues to the circumstances of Olson's death were quickly erased. Telling the truth selectively, Lashbrook informed the police that Olson "suffered from ulcers." (He had, in fact, once taken a leave of absence from work because of them.) That was the extent of his cooperation with authorities outside the agency. Within a few days the police had been persuaded to quietly drop their investigation in the interest of national security. Teams of CIA security officers went everywhere that Olson had been, covering tracks.

CIA Director Allen Dulles told those with a need to know that it had all been an honest, if terrible, mistake. No one had wanted to kill Olson. No harm had been done to the country or to anyone in power. The only victim was Frank Olson, and there were other biochemists who could make poison lipstick.

The CIA's upper echelon agreed: a mistake had been made. The mistake was not that the agency had killed someone, but that it had killed someone who could be traced back to the agency. Gottlieb was instructed to start an improved LSD testing program with more anonymous prey. The new, unsuspecting bodies were street prostitutes (and their low-level businessman clients), petty thieves, homosexuals, gamblers, and drifters; powerless people whose odd behavior and potential deaths would cause little or no fuss. Instead of spiking a cognac at an exclusive retreat, CIA agents dropped acid into watered-down drinks (perhaps using their new sleight of hand skills) at two-bit bars, strip clubs, and at a private bordello that the agency ran in San Francisco. They then followed their victims and recorded their reactions. This testing program went on for ten years. For at least ten years after that LSD was used in covert operations, until more dependable interrogation and brainwashing methods were developed. Ethics played no part in the CIA's decision to stop using LSD.

The CIA inspector general reviewed the death of Frank Olson and recommended that Sid Gottlieb be reprimanded. Allen Dulles reviewed the recommendation and—apparently not wishing to hurt a man who showed initiative—wrote a mildly chastising letter criticizing Gottlieb's "poor judgment." He then ordered that even this slap on the wrist be kept out of Gottlieb's personnel file so that it wouldn't harm his future career.

The strange death of Frank Olson made headlines, but it was forgotten. Sid Gottlieb attended Frank Olson's funeral, contributed to his memorial fund, and visited Mrs. Olson at home—which confused her, since she had no idea who he was. Alice Olson was told that her husband died of a "classified illness," and then was later told that he had either fallen or jumped out a window for reasons unknown. She didn't believe either story, but she kept her silence. The agency saw to it that she received two-thirds of her husband's salary as a pension.

When Sid Gottlieb retired from the CIA in 1973, Director Richard Helms ordered the destruction of virtually all documents mentioning the MK-Ultra program. But in December 1974 the *New York Times* broke the story of the CIA's mind-control experiments. That prompted investigations by both a congressional committee (the Church Committee) and a presidential commission (the Rockefeller Commission) into the domestic activities of the CIA, the FBI, and the intelligence-related agencies of the military. In June 1975 both the committee and the commission revealed that at least one subject of these experiments had died after ingesting LSD.

Alice Olson and her three children, now grown, realized that that subject was Frank Olson. They went on national television and told his story. Subsequent digging, under the provisions of the Freedom of Information Act, turned up some eight thousand pages of secret CIA internal memoranda and documents about Olson and MK-Ultra that Helms had somehow missed destroying.

In 1976 Congress passed a bill authorizing a settlement of $750,000 to the Olson family in return for their dropping a pending lawsuit. The family was also invited to the White House, where they received a personal apology from President Gerald Ford. Alice Olson later had a women's drug and alcohol recovery center in Frederick named in her honor.

The United States government's quest for control over human behavior piled up an international body count, but its victims remain obscure. No one knows how many others suffered fates similar to Frank Olson. Few care. If willful ignorance is a form of mind control, then the government appears, in the end, to have gotten what it wanted.

# The Peace Chief

THE YEAR 1864 WAS A TERRIBLE ONE FOR THE SOUTHERN Cheyenne.

The tribe had once claimed hundreds of square miles of prairie, stretching across most of what is now eastern Colorado and western Kansas. It was an enormous tract of land, prime hunting ground for bison and antelope. But white settlers were pushing in from the east, slaughtering the wildlife and transforming grassland into farms and ranches. To the west lay the impassable Rocky Mountains—where gold had been discovered. As the Civil War neared its end, white settlers, fortune-seekers, and soldiers began pouring into the region. With the coming of the railroads, their numbers would only increase.

One Southern Cheyenne who tried to make the best of this bad situation was Make-ta-vatah, known to the whites as Black Kettle. He was a "peace chief," elected by the tribe for both his courage and his concern for others' well-being. He was, by contemporary accounts, calm and intelligent, a leader with integrity, and a politician who sought progress through compromise. He recognized the military and numerical superiority of the whites and understood that cooperation with them was the best— and perhaps only—way for his people to survive.

Unfortunately, by 1864 cooperation was not embraced by most Southern Cheyenne. Nor, for that matter, was it the choice of most whites.

Young Cheyenne warriors attacked stagecoaches and outlying ranches. In retaliation, whites killed Cheyenne warriors. To escape the bloodshed, Black Kettle led his band of peace seekers to southeastern Colorado, where they set up a village on the banks of Sand Creek. They surrendered their guns and horses at nearby Fort Lyons, in effect becoming prisoners of war, to show their friendly intentions and qualify for promised winter provisions. Federal officers assured Black Kettle that his people would be safe from U.S. Army attack as long as they stayed in their village.

West of Black Kettle's village lay Denver, an overgrown mining town and a hotbed of anti-Indian sentiment. One of its most fanatical firebrands was "Fighting Parson" John Chivington, a Methodist minister who had his eye on a congressional seat in the fall elections. He recognized a good campaign issue in the Southern Cheyenne and loudly demanded their wholesale annihilation. The territorial governor, also anxious to appear tough on the Indians but lacking qualified manpower, recklessly gave Chivington command of the Third Colorado Volunteers, a company of rough men who, like Chivington, viewed the Indians as vermin to be exterminated. As the summer waned, they set out to confront the Southern Cheyenne.

They didn't have much luck. The Southern Cheyenne rebels were scattered over a vast territory. They wisely waged guerrilla warfare, raiding a house here, an outpost there, offering Chivington little opportunity for battle and glory. September passed into October, then November. With the Colorado Volunteers' enlistments about to expire, taunted as "The Bloodless Third" by the newspapers, Chivington's troops made their way back toward Denver—on a route that would take them through Sand Creek.

Chivington needed to kill Indians. The village at Sand Creek had about seven hundred of them.

Black Kettle was surprised to hear screams at dawn on November 29. He walked out of his lodge and saw Chivington's men approaching the village from two sides. Black Kettle, who respected rules and agreements, called to his people not to be afraid. Above him fluttered a white flag of truce and a large American flag, a gift he'd received at one of his peace parlays. Don't be afraid of the soldiers, Black Kettle said. The white men promised we will not be harmed. Chivington's troops leveled their weapons and opened fire.

Chivington estimated that his men killed a half-thousand Indians in the next hour. On his orders, they took no prisoners. Any Indian attempting to surrender was put to death. Women and children were followed as they tried to escape, shot and scalped. Pregnant women were cut open; little children had their brains beaten out. The dead and dying had their genitals hacked off. One soldier bragged of cutting out a squaw's heart and impaling it on a spear.

Black Kettle's wife was shot nine times while she lay on the ground. Miraculously, she survived. So did Black Kettle. Given the Indians' unpreparedness and Chivington's overwhelming firepower, it's amazing that every Cheyenne wasn't killed. Yet despite the Fighting Parson's boast, the death toll was nearer to 250 than 500. Most were women and children.

The survivors lost everything but their lives. They dragged themselves eastward across the barren, freezing prairie, eventually finding shelter with the neighboring Kiowa tribe. Chivington headed west to Denver and exhibited his bloody human trophies to cheering crowds. The citizens held a parade in his honor.

Black Kettle was not dead. Nor, amazingly, was his desire for peaceful coexistence. "Although wrongs have been done to me I live in hope," he told a congressional investigating committee in 1865. "Although the troops have struck us, we throw it all behind and are glad to meet you in peace and friendship."

For a brief period it appeared as if Black Kettle's spirit of good will might prevail. Both the regular army and Washington officials were horrified by Chivington's actions, which the press had dubbed the Sand Creek Massacre. The parades in Denver were replaced by a Peace Commission. Chivington hung up his battle spurs and his political ambitions, if only to avoid military prosecution. Black Kettle received 320 acres in compensation for his injuries.

But the peace chief spoke for fewer Southern Cheyenne than before, and not just because of Chivington's bullets. The 320 acres did not solve the problem of land ownership.

The whites kept coming. Many of the surviving Cheyenne felt that if the tribe was going to be annihilated, it was better to go down fighting than to be slowly starved to death. Ranches, wagon trains, and the construction crews for the new railroads became targets for revenge. Angry braves roamed the old ancestral lands hunting bison, stealing supplies and horses, and occasionally killing whites.

Still, Black Kettle counseled peace. He took his people to a new reservation in Kansas in 1866. In 1867 he moved them again, this time to a reserve in Indian Territory, which is now Oklahoma. The lands were poor; the people suffered. Disease and malnutrition wasted the Southern Cheyenne, but the whites had no more patience for Indian problems. Instead, they talked of putting an end to "Indian treachery" once and for all. Veteran cavalry troops arriving daily from the east were an ominous sign. Black Kettle knew trouble was coming.

The Office of Indian Affairs knew it too. In November 1868 they put out the word to all peaceable Indians to head south to Fort Cobb, deep inside Indian Territory. Once there, the Indians would be allowed to surrender officially, pitch their winter camps, and collect provisions. Those who obeyed would be out of the war zone; those who didn't would be considered hostile.

Black Kettle led his followers to the Washita River, where they pitched camp about a hundred miles west of the fort. He rode eastward and offered to surrender, anxious to move his people away from the troops. But the commanding officer refused; some of Black Kettle's young braves were suspected of joining the rebels. Black Kettle told the officer that he no longer controlled everyone in his band, but that those who remained wanted peace and security. "I would be glad to move all my people down this way," he said. "I could then keep them all quietly near camp." The officer sent him away.

While Black Kettle was talking, three columns of armed U.S. cavalry were converging, pincer-style, on the Washita. In the lead was Lieutenant Colonel George Armstrong Custer, eager to atone for a bad summer campaign in Kansas. He'd failed to catch the elusive Southern Cheyenne raiders and at one point he'd had his command suspended when it was learned he had abandoned his troops to visit his wife. He did not take public humiliation lightly.

Unknown to the Office of Indian Affairs, the War Department had its own plan for the encamped Indians. Its plan was to kill them. Custer's cavalry would wait until the tribes were settled in their winter lodges, then attack. All of the Indians' possessions would be seized or destroyed; those who survived the raids would be deported to reservations. It was a bloody, brutal plan, but it would be effective. There would be no more Indian raids because there would be no more Indians.

The Southern Cheyenne camped along the Washita suspected nothing. It's doubtful that Black Kettle could even have imagined such coldhearted treachery as was then closing in around him. He and his people didn't want to fight. They wanted to surrender. "I do not feel afraid to go among the white men," he had told the commander at Fort Cobb, "because I feel them to be my friends."

Almost four years to the day after the Sand Creek Massacre, armed troops again descended at dawn on Black Kettle's sleeping villagers. Within the first few minutes, Custer and his men killed over a hundred Southern Cheyenne. Again, a white flag of truce flew over the carnage. Again, most of the victims were women and children.

This time Black Kettle and his wife did not escape. Both were shot repeatedly at the river's edge. Custer's mounted troops trampled the aged Indians' bullet-ridden bodies, crushing them into the cold Oklahoma mud.

Unlike the massacre at Sand Creek, the savage slaughter at the Washita was praised as a military victory. Custer was hailed as a hero and achieved instant fame as an Indian fighter. The surviving Southern Cheyenne were rounded up and exiled to a reservation. The raids in Colorado and Kansas ceased.

Washita's lesson was as old as warfare, and one that Black Kettle would never have understood: Kill everyone who disagrees with you, and you will have peace.

# No Laughing Matter

IT WAS A GRUESOME DISCOVERY, EVEN FOR SUCH A PLACE as the Tombs in New York City. The guard making his morning rounds found Horace Wells sprawled on the floor of his cell, dead in a pool of his own congealed blood. Wells had just turned thirty-three.

A few years earlier, that would have seemed preposterous, even impossible. Fortune had always favored Horace Wells. Well-educated, the son of respectable, socially prominent parents, he had taught himself dentistry and built a prestigious practice. His home was Hartford, capital of Connecticut, and among his sizable clientele were many of that state's most powerful families, including the governor's. He mixed in the right social circles, made good money, married well, and was admired by those who worked with him.

So how did Horace Wells end up dead on the stone floor of America's most notorious prison?

Horace Wells practiced medicine in a world of pain. Anesthesia did not yet exist in the dirty, crowded surgery rooms of 1844. The only way to reduce suffering was to cut, saw, and stitch with as much speed as possible. Even the comparatively minor, routine dental surgery performed by Wells was an ordeal for the patient, to be undergone only when the agony of disease or injury became unbearable.

All physicians were affected by knowing they would have to cause pain to help their patients, but Horace Wells took it harder than most. He was sensitive, spiritual, even romantic. Although several ways to eliminate pain had been tried—asphyxiation, freezing, burning, bleeding, alcohol, hypnotism, narcotics—Wells rejected them as haphazard and dangerous. Anesthesia caused more agony than it relieved. It was the province of quacks.

What Wells and the rest of the medical community did not know was that for the past half century two perfectly good anesthetics had already been available, and both were in widespread use. However, they were being used to get people stoned.

Nitrous oxide and ether were manufactured gasses that had been inhaled at public "frolics" or for private pleasure since the early nineteenth century. Traveling exhibitors would fill leather bags with one or the other, invite male volunteers onstage (women were forbidden), then have them suck down the vapors while their noses were pinched shut. Almost immediately, the men would break into spontaneous dancing and fighting, usually while laughing hysterically. It was a popular after-dinner entertainment. The drugs were called "laughing gas" by the public, "exhilarating gas" by the more genteel.

A nitrous oxide frolic occurred in Hartford in December 1844 and Horace Wells attended. By chance, the young man seated next to him was a volunteer. After jumping around the stage and running into several heavy pieces of furniture, he returned to his seat with his legs bloody and badly bruised. When Wells pointed out his injuries to him, the young man was flabbergasted; he couldn't recall hurting himself. More important, Wells realized, the man *felt no pain*. This was impossible, according to the teachings of nineteenth-century medicine. Perhaps that's why self-schooled Horace Wells was among the first to notice it.

Anxious and excited, Wells had the exhibitor bring a bag of the gas to his office first thing the next morning. He inhaled it and then had another Hartford dentist yank out one of his molars. He felt no pain. "It's the greatest discovery ever made!" he cried after he'd regained his senses. "I didn't feel so much as the prick of a pin!"

Wells immediately began making the gas and putting it to use in his dental practice. Over the next few weeks he gave nitrous oxide to more than a dozen patients; nearly all felt no pain. Wells was elated. Here at last was the long-awaited universal pain-killer, an end not only to patient suffering, but to Horace Wells's angst as well.

Wells had to prove the benefits of nitrous oxide to the world, but how? There was no FDA to confer legitimacy in 1844. Wells decided to travel to Boston—the haughty nucleus of a very haughty profession—and stage a demonstration in one of its famed teaching hospitals.

He needed the aid of an insider to enter this elite neighborhood, and he found one in William Thomas

Green Morton, a former student and business partner of Wells who had gone to Boston to further his medical education. Morton was a smooth talker, and by late January 1845 he'd persuaded one of his professors to allow Wells's demonstration. It was an impressive accomplishment for Morton: Wells would perform before the surgical class at Massachusetts General Hospital, one of the most prestigious medical institutions in the country. The spectators in the operating amphitheater, however, seemed more annoyed than impressed. Who was this tooth-puller from Connecticut to waste the valuable time of Harvard doctors in training? A dentist was going to use a party gas to defeat surgical pain? Maybe he would also flap his arms and fly to the moon. . . .

What happened next has never been satisfactorily explained. Perhaps the patient received too little gas or perhaps he wasn't completely unconscious when the extraction began. For whatever reason, the man cried out as his tooth was pulled. That reaction was more than enough for Wells's hostile audience. The students howled from their bleacher seats, laughing, hissing, booing him from the room. Wells was denounced throughout Boston as a fraud. He valiantly remained in the city for another three weeks, pleading for a second chance, but no one wanted anything more to do with Horace Wells.

Devastated by his failure, Wells returned to Hartford and resumed his practice, only occasionally performing painless extractions. His heart wasn't in it. He sank into a depression, then a deep despondency. After a month of melancholy, he closed his office for a leave of absence and a much-needed rest.

In Boston, the medical establishment returned to business as usual. Having discredited Wells, America's doctors promptly forgot about him and his nitrous oxide.

One doctor did not. Charles Jackson, a chemist as well as a physician, had been in the amphitheater during Wells's presentation, and he'd recognized that what Wells was saying was true. It was also true that a man's reputation could easily be destroyed in the anesthesia snake pit. Jackson was no idealist; he wanted fame but he also valued his career. He decided that the best way to test gas anesthesia was through a front man, someone who could sell the idea and take the fall if necessary, someone with less to lose—like a dentist. He thought of William Thomas Green Morton.

Morton was not brilliant, but he had the right connections and he had few scruples; how few, Jackson would soon discover. He obviously had no qualms about stealing his old teacher's idea. More than anything, Morton liked the idea of being rich, and with a track record of bad business deals stretching back years, he wanted to be rich quick.

On the pretense of repaying some old debts, Morton traveled to Hartford and visited Wells. It was actually a fact-finding mission, for he grilled Wells on how to make and use nitrous oxide. Wells, suspecting nothing and eager to spread the word, told Morton all he knew. Ironically, he suggested that Morton contact Charles Jackson back in Boston, a chemist who had the skills and equipment necessary to produce the gas.

Morton returned to Boston and briefed Jackson. Jackson told Morton to forget nitrous oxide; it was too costly and too troublesome to produce. Instead he gave Morton a supply of ether, the other laughing gas, which Wells had rejected as too potentially dangerous for his patients. Jackson and Morton weren't as picky. Using the instructions he had wheedled out of Wells, Morton quickly began anesthetizing every creature he could get his hands on: his goldfish, his dog, then himself. He recruited volunteers from the seedier streets of Boston, had them sniff the vapor, then yanked out their teeth. The stuff worked. Crazy Horace Wells had been right after all.

Unlike Wells, who insisted that anesthesia be "as free as the air we breathe" and who had rushed to make its properties known, Jackson and Morton were in no hurry to demonstrate their discovery publicly. Ether, after all, was a cheaply made, commonly available, industrial chemical. Once the word was out, everyone would be able to use it. How would that profit Jackson and Morton?

Morton came up with a plan. He had Jackson add some perfume to the ether and, presto, it became a mysterious new wonder drug, Letheon Gas. Morton had it patented, then placed ads in medical magazines and hired agents to hawk franchises and licenses for this marvelous new discovery. Not only would people have to pay Morton (and the shadowy Jackson) to purchase the gas, they'd have to pay for the right to use it. Boston's medical establishment cringed at the ballyhoo, but what could you expect from a dentist?

It's not known who suggested the idea—it might very well have been Morton—but a demonstration of Letheon was arranged in the same amphitheater, before the same professor, as Wells's demonstration nearly two years earlier. The crowd was, if anything, more hostile than before, but the glib Morton pulled off a flawless demonstration. This time gas was used—not for a mere tooth extraction, but to successfully anesthetize a patient while a goiter was cut from his neck. "It is no humbug," the professor declared. Massachusetts General Hospital, suddenly proud of its former student, threw its considerable weight behind Morton.

Jackson was left out in the cold. He realized too late that Morton wasn't about to give credit, or money, to anyone but himself. Furious, Jackson fired off a series of scathing broadsides to every major newspaper and professional journal he could think of, denouncing Morton and revealing that the discoverer of anesthesia was actually another man—Charles Jackson. His public rancor only served to expose the fraud that Letheon was nothing more than perfumed ether. Within three months of Morton's demonstration, the leading hospitals of New York, London, and Paris were anesthetizing patients and performing operations with the standard industrial-grade gas.

Back in Hartford, Wells's blissful ignorance was short-lived. Only three days after Morton's successful demonstration, Morton wrote to Wells and arrogantly offered him the chance to sell Letheon franchises. Out of sheer wickedness, he also included Boston newspaper clippings hailing himself as the discoverer of anesthesia. Horrified, Wells dashed off a series of angry letters to the Boston Medical Surgical Journal, denouncing Letheon as a fraud and demanding an apology from his former student and the recognition that he, Wells, was the rightful discoverer of anesthesia. Morton and Jackson stopped attacking each other long enough to fire back: Wells was a failure, nitrous oxide was a joke.

Getting nowhere in Boston, Wells traveled to Paris to present his case before its Academy of Sciences and Medicine, the most prestigious medical body in the world. He was too late. Jackson, quick and ruthless, had immediately written to the academy with all the particulars and details of Morton's successful demonstration—without mentioning Morton, of course. Now all of Paris hailed Jackson as the discoverer of anesthesia. The academy had the dated, postmarked letter to prove it.

Wells fought back, lecturing in Paris and London, asserting his primacy over Jackson before returning to the States and resuming his battle with Morton. This would be a much tougher contest. While Hartford rallied behind its native son, powerful Massachusetts General Hospital stubbornly defended Morton's claims. There was more than local pride at stake for Massachusetts General, which was locked in a fight with Philadelphia's Pennsylvania Hospital to be recognized as America's premiere medical center. Being the birthplace of anesthesia was a terrific coup. Massachusetts General stood behind Morton long after they might otherwise have booted him out the back door.

As the summer of 1847 waned, Wells had resumed his role as the Johnny Appleseed of nitrous oxide, offering his services as an anesthesiologist to every doctor and dentist in Hartford. Jackson was still trying to claim ether as his own discovery in Paris. Morton was in Washington lobbying Congress to have his patent enforced. Something had to give, and that something was Horace Wells.

Only three years after his momentous discovery, Wells left Hartford and his family and moved to New York City's Greenwich Village. The reason remains unclear.

He claimed that he wanted to start a new practice in a new town, but it seems more likely that Horace Wells was running away. He was tired of the rancor and bickering and of a battle that Morton, with the backing of Massachusetts General Hospital, seemed destined to win. Perhaps, too, his years of experimental gas-sniffing had finally unhinged his mind. "My brain is on fire," he wrote home in 1848. "I am fast becoming a deranged man."

The effects of prolonged nitrous oxide use were not known in the mid-nineteenth century, nor were the effects known of sniffing ether or a new anesthetic, chloroform. In fact, all three were horribly dangerous, and all were readily available in Manhattan. Without the anchor of family and friends, obviously feeling sorry and alone, Horace Wells celebrated his thirty-third birthday by getting tanked on chloroform.

Intoxicated, Wells ran out of his apartment and onto Broadway, where he repeatedly threw sulfuric acid on the clothes of passing women, apparently believing them to be prostitutes and that by burning their clothes he would force them out of his neighborhood. When Wells came to his senses several hours later, he was in jail.

The guards felt sorry for this well-dressed, soft-spoken gentleman so obviously out of place and miserable in his cell. In some respects the nineteenth century was more humane than our own, and when Wells asked one of the guards if he would escort him back to his apartment to fetch his shaving kit, the guard agreed. Wells not only retrieved his straight razor, he pocketed a bottle of chloroform as well.

That night, Horace Wells wrote farewell letters to his friends and family. "I cannot live and keep my reason," he said. "Great God! has it come to this? Is it not all a dream?" He draped a towel over his face and poured the chloroform onto it. He breathed deeply. All the hurt, the embarrassment, the injustice of the last three years melted away. Floating on his chemical cloud, Wells picked up the straight razor and carefully, repeatedly slashed his left thigh down to the bone, severing his femoral artery. Blood poured onto the floor. Horace Wells slowly grew weaker, then died. There was no pain.

He had no way of knowing that the Academy of Sciences and Medicine had just reversed itself and now publicly hailed Horace Wells as the true discoverer of anesthetic gasses.

As it turned out, the academy was still wrong. Wells wasn't the first to discover gas anesthesia after all. The honor actually belonged to an obscure Georgia country doctor named Crawford Long, who had stumbled upon the technique after a gas frolic in 1842, more than two years before Wells would do exactly the same thing. Unlike Wells, Long was isolated by geography and in no hurry to save the world. Long anesthetized patients when he could and carefully recorded his experiments. He outlived not only Wells, but Jackson and Morton, passing away after delivering a baby on a house call, a beloved and respected man.

Jackson and Morton, on the other hand, had the pleasure of killing each other. After three petitions to Congress and an interview with President James Buchanan, Morton was declared anesthesia's true discoverer. Jackson responded with a litany of lawsuits that kept Morton in court for years, eventually driving him to financial ruin.

Meanwhile, the gasses they had inhaled for so long were taking their toll. Jackson's accusations grew more bizarre. He now claimed to have invented the telegraph as well as anesthesia. Morton spent time detoxifying in a mental institution, then returned to Manhattan to defend himself against a new charge by Jackson. He collapsed and died in an apoplectic fit. Jackson, triumphant, went to visit Morton's grave, saw the elegant obelisk erected by the trustees of Massachusetts General Hospital, and lost his mind. He died after seven years in an insane asylum. His gravestone, in the same cemetery as Morton's, is inscribed with a lengthy polemic against the unjustness of his life.

Horace Wells was bankrupt when he committed suicide. All of his medical equipment and household furniture had to be sold to pay his creditors. Ashamed at his failure, he asked to be buried "in the most secret manner possible" at the jail in which he took his own life. Thankfully, his friends and family ignored this last request. His body was shipped home to Hartford and interred with dignity.

More than a hundred years after the death of the last anesthesia warrior, Hartford's citizens organized a campaign to have Horace Wells honored on a postage stamp. In 1993, after ten years of petitions, phone calls, and countless letters to Washington, the citizen's advisory committee of the U.S. Postal Service reviewed the proposal—and rejected it.

The matter, they explained, was still too controversial.

# Dog Gone Shame

THE BLOODIEST WAR OF THE TWENTIETH CENTURY WASN'T fought in the fields of France. It didn't stain the steppes of Russia or sully the rice patties of Southeast Asia. It was fought here, in America, on the shortgrass prairie of Nebraska, the intermountain meadows of Colorado, and the high plains of New Mexico.

The battle is ongoing. And from almost the first shot, you've been paying for it.

This unfinished Armageddon already has a victor: the American cowboy, icon of the West and hero of popular mythology. The loser, as might be expected, is less glamorous. It's the prairie dog.

The prairie dog? Even more American than the cowboy, found nowhere else on earth, these highly social, burrowing animals (cousins of the ground squirrel) live in organized, underground tunnel communities called "towns," bark like dogs (hence their name), eat brush and grass, and are generally plump, furry, and cute.

Mass animal extinctions in America are nothing new. Six to seven million bison were slaughtered in the late nineteenth century, as were hundreds of millions of passenger pigeons. But their body counts are puny compared to the prairie dog's. Even by the most conservative estimate, 4.5 *billion* prairie dogs have been killed in the past century, shrinking its population, according to one study, by 99.75 percent. That's equal to killing every single human being in America except for the citizens of Columbus, Ohio.

In Texas, for example, the prairie dog population has dropped from eight hundred million to less than two million. It's dropped because prairie dogs have been poisoned, shot, stomped, clubbed, roasted, drowned, garroted, gassed, torn apart, run over, and blown up, an average of nearly twenty-three thousand a day, every day, since 1900.

And that's just one state.

The prairie dog must have done something awful to deserve this fate. Perhaps it carried some dread disease. Or maybe it was a ravager of crops, a furry locust that would have chewed its way through the Breadbasket of the Nation and left us starving and helpless—were it not for our fearless cowboys.

Actually, the prairie dog did nothing wrong. It threatened no one's safety, not even any animal's. What it did threaten was the profits of America's powerful livestock industry. And for that, it has been mercilessly and unceasingly butchered.

When the twentieth century dawned, billions of prairie dogs lived on the great semiarid and shortgrass prairies that stretched from midway across Kansas, Nebraska, Oklahoma, Texas, and the Dakotas west to the Rocky Mountains. This endless expanse of brush and grass—more than seven hundred million acres—was dubbed the "Great American desert" by early settlers, who considered it worthless because it was too dry for agriculture. However, it was ideal for prairie dogs and for the thousands of other animal and plant species that were adapted to it.

Prairie dogs were the anchor of the Great Plains ecosystem. Their towns were biological oases, teeming with life. Burrowing prairie dogs churned up dirt, circulating the soil, spreading seeds, and fostering the growth of over eighty species of plants. Their endless networks of tunnels allowed precious water to sink beneath the hardpan, where plant roots could tap it. Nibbling prairie dogs kept the vegetation young and more nutritious for the larger animals that came to the towns to feed.

Coronado's sixteenth-century expedition across this grassy Eden reported prairie dogs in "infinite numbers." One prairie dog town in western Texas spread 100 miles in one direction and 250 in the other—an area larger than Rhode Island, Connecticut, New Hampshire, and Massachusetts combined.

Then the American cowboy arrived. Unlike the farmer, he recognized that the shortgrass prairie could be exploited, for livestock grazing. But its scattered vegetation meant that each cow and sheep would need many acres of grazing land to reach a profitable weight. That could only happen if the prairie was first cleared—of Indians, animal predators, and animal competitors.

Most of this dirty work was done by the 1890s. The Indians were either dead or banished to reservations. The predators and competitors—the wolf, bison, elk, bear, and coyote—were just dead. Only one native mammal was left in numbers that threatened livestock ranchers—the prairie dog.

It bears repeating that the same prairie dog habits that helped native grazing animals would also have helped the cowboy's livestock. Billions of prairie dogs had shared the ecosystem with millions of bison, deer, and antelope. They could have shared it as easily with cows and sheep—if the cows and sheep had been grazed in numbers suited to the environment.

That "if," however, was too much to ask of the American livestock industry. Fewer animals meant less money. Cowboys didn't become wealthy ranchers by making less money.

Stockmen herded tens of millions of cows and sheep onto the prairie. Livestock stripped the vegetation to stubble. Forage vanished. The prairie dog, no longer a cog in a balanced ecosystem, became a competitor by necessity. The ranchers attacked with murderous fury—the prairie dog war was on.

Victory proved elusive at first. Prairie dogs were surprisingly adaptable and fertile. Though the ranchers shot them, trapped them, strangled them with nooses, drowned them in their burrows, and blew up their towns with dynamite—killing millions—they would not go away.

The prairie dog probably could have held its ground against the ranchers, but events far from the prairie sealed its fate. The tide turned when C. S. Merriam, director of the U.S. Biological Survey, declared that prairie dogs decreased land productivity by 50 to 75 percent. Where he got those figures no one knows; they were broadly inaccurate, to put it mildly. But Congress was impressed, and in 1909 it appropriated funds to the USDA for "experiments and demonstrations in destroying noxious animals." With tax money from the federal treasury and the tactical support of countless range managers and county agents, the ranchers suddenly had the prairie dog on the short end of a very big stick.

Mass poisoning was the preferred method for killing the most prairie dogs for the least money. Government agents traveled to large prairie dog towns and seeded them with grain soaked in strychnine, arsenic, and sodium cyanide. Ranchers reportedly helped things along by taking prairie dogs infected with plague and turning them loose in the colonies.

The results of these efforts were impressive, if not astonishing. In 1908, for example, a biologist traveled forty miles through southern New Mexico and reported that the area was one giant prairie dog town, with an estimated 6.4 million inhabitants. Fifty years later, workers from the Museum of Southwestern Biology traveled the same region. There were no prairie dogs.

Through the teens, twenties, and thirties the killing continued. Exterminating prairie dogs helped keep America employed during the Great Depression; in some years more than 125,000 men worked to spread poison over twenty million acres. After World War II a new weapon appeared in the government's arsenal, sodium monofluoroacetate—popularly called Compound 1080—developed by Nazi Germany as a chemical warfare agent. Less than $1/500$ of an ounce would kill a grown man. Federal and state agencies broadcast tons of grain soaked in it from trucks, helicopters, and airplanes.

All the great prairie dog colonies were destroyed by the 1970s. Billions of gophers, turtles, rabbits, mice, and seed-eating birds died along with the prairie dogs, as did the badgers, ferrets, foxes, bobcats, coyotes, and eagles that ate their toxic bodies. More than eight hundred thousand square miles of the West were poisoned.

Washington gradually reduced its funding for mass killings—in part because most prairie dogs were now dead—but maintained programs of "spot treatments" through agencies like the Forest Service and the Bureau of Land Management. When Compound 1080 was banned by the EPA, zinc phosphide replaced it. This poison inflicted a slow and painful death, so prairie dogs in national parks and other public areas were instead suffocated in their burrows with gas or smoke bombs. It took more time and cost more money, but it kept the writhing, spasming, dying prairie dogs underground and out of sight.

Perhaps the most amazing thing about the extermination of the prairie dog is that it has never ended. South Dakota and Wyoming, for example, still encourage anyone with a gun to kill prairie dogs any time, virtually anywhere, as many as they like. Counties and townships in Kansas have the authority to track down and kill prairie dogs and make the landowner pay a fee for this service. On most public lands you don't even need to ask permission to blow away prairie dogs; just drive in and start blasting.

Shooting prairie dogs requires no arduous trekking, no special hunting gear; it really takes very little effort.

Sportsmen can drive their air-conditioned pickups or vans to prairie dog towns following directions provided by county agents and local chambers of commerce. Hunters who appreciate comfort can tow flatbed shooting platforms outfitted with swivel chairs, adjustable clamps to hold and aim the guns, and an awning to provide shade if the afternoon sun is too hot. They lazily pick off prairie dogs as the animals come out of their burrows.

Particularly curious is the continued slaughter of prairie dogs on U.S. public lands, those parklike places with the big NATIONAL GRASSLAND and NATURAL AREA signs out front. Public lands comprise roughly one-third of America and belong to everyone, in theory, yet many of them are grazed by livestock. Public lands ranchers—the only people who benefit from public-land prairie dog exterminations—embody only .0088 percent of America's citizens. Did anyone ever ask you, the other 99.9912 percent, if you'd rather have cows than prairie dogs on your public lands?

Perhaps this perpetual butchery would be understandable if the prairie dog were, in fact, a threat. Yet the U.S. Departments of Interior and Agriculture have known for decades that prairie dogs are not, and have never been, a significant danger to ranchers, farmers, or anyone else. Why the continuing carnage?

The answer lies in the cozy relationship between America's politicians and its livestock industry, a surprisingly powerful—and generous—special interest. County and state governments in the prairie region and the federal government in Washington routinely yield to the views of cattlemen and ranchers. And the prevailing view among them—ignoring ample evidence to the contrary—

is that prairie dogs are an economic menace that needs to be eliminated.

Prairie dog killing enjoyed renewed popularity under the Reagan and Bush administrations. Over 450,000 acres of prairie dog habitat was poisoned in just one spot treatment in 1983 on South Dakota's Pine Ridge Reservation, at a cost to the taxpayer of $6.2 million. Yet at the same time prairie dogs were enjoying a rare—if ironic—victory. One of their predators, the black-footed ferret, became an endangered species. It had nearly been starved out of existence, and since its sole food source had been the prairie dog, people began to ask uncomfortable questions.

In October 1994 the prairie dog itself was proposed as a category-2 endangered species. Category 2 is the lowest rung on the near-extinction ladder, but it was too much to ask of the ranching community. Anything that might restrict killing prairie dogs was unacceptable, and the livestock industry let Washington know it. The Fish and Wildlife Service reviewed the proposal, solemnly agreed that the prairie-dog-driven Great Plains ecosystem was in serious trouble—and rejected it. The prairie dog slaughter went on, unhindered.

Livestock industry apologists have made much of a new, "humane" approach to prairie dog removal—vacuuming. A truck designed for cleaning furnaces and sewer lines arrives at a prairie dog town, giant hoses are snaked into the burrows, and the inhabitants are sucked out of the ground. This new technique makes little difference to the adult prairie dogs—who are killed later anyway—but the babies are taken alive and sold to exotic animal fanciers in the United States and Japan.

Old-time ranchers are more enamored of another new technology, the backpackable mini-flamethrower. It first pumps combustible gas into the prairie dogs' burrow system, then ignites it. Everything underground—prairie dogs, turtles, gophers, snakes, weasels, badgers—is roasted alive.

Prairie dogs are barbecued and vacuumed today for the same reason they were blown up a hundred years ago—as a scapegoat for livestock overgrazing. No one knows how many are left. Estimates range from several hundred thousand to several million. Everyone agrees that their numbers are dwindling.

On the flip side, there are more beef cattle in the United States than ever before. The shortgrass prairie— what's left of it—is rapidly becoming a monotonous ecological desert, populated exclusively by livestock and their ranchers. From a short-term business perspective, things couldn't be better.

Some small prairie dog colonies will undoubtedly be allowed to survive on public lands as a token population, providing sportsmen with live targets and cattlemen with a convenient villain that will justify continuing subsidies from Uncle Sam.

It's already too late to expect much more than that for the prairie dog. With politicians unwilling to act and the public too uninformed to care, this holocaust isn't ending any time soon.

# 7

# Human Product

ACCORDING TO WHAT RECORDS SURVIVE, EBENEZER CADE was an unremarkably average, middle-aged man. If anything, he was healthier than average. He worked as a cement mixer for a construction company, a job that required strength and stamina. And he most likely would have lived out his days in obscurity if he hadn't suffered an unfortunate auto accident in March 1945. Extremely unfortunate—for Ebenezer was working at the secret Oak Ridge, Tennessee, nuclear weapons plant at the time and was taken to the Oak Ridge Army Hospital for treatment. His bad luck—and the bad luck of hundreds of others—was only beginning.

Ebenezer's accident left him with multiple bone fractures so severe that the doctors at Oak Ridge believed he would die. Their diagnosis was as fateful as it was flawed; it seems in fact to have been based on wishful thinking. Certain doctors at Oak Ridge were hoping to find a patient like Ebenezer Cade, someone organically sound but not expected to live. They hastily concluded that Ebenezer met their criteria. While he lay helpless in his hospital bed—trusting, we can imagine, that the doctors had his best interests in mind—one of the Oak Ridge physicians walked up to his bedside, stuck a needle in his arm, and injected him with plutonium-239.

Plutonium is a highly radioactive metal with unusual properties. Since it emits only alpha particles (which cannot readily penetrate human skin) it can be safely carried around for brief periods in something like a hypodermic syringe. However, should plutonium somehow find its way beneath the skin and into the human body—say, by being injected into a vein—it can be deadly. It will also stay around a long, long time. Plutonium has a half-life of twenty-four thousand years.

To understand why Ebenezer was made radioactive, it helps to remember what was known and unknown as of March 1945. The United States was still building the nuclear weapons that would later destroy Hiroshima and Nagasaki. The atomic bomb had not yet been exploded, and no one knew the metabolism and toxicology of long-lived radioactive elements. The Atomic Energy Commission (AEC) needed answers: How much radiation could a weapons worker be exposed to and survive? Were there any physical markers? What effects would different doses of radiation have on human beings?

Ebenezer, although he didn't know it, had become a human guinea pig for nuclear weapons safety research.

The doctors were careful not to inject Ebenezer with so much plutonium that it would cause immediate effects. They didn't want to give him radiation poisoning—at least not instantly—and they certainly didn't want to tip him off that something improper was going on. Instead, they calculated that about five micrograms of plutonium would be enough to leave a radioactive trail through his circulatory and digestive system, which they could then track. As the radiation settled into his organs and bone marrow, Ebenezer would be at considerable risk of developing cancer, but the doctors had convinced themselves that Ebenezer would die in days, not years.

Ebenezer was christened "HP-12"—Human Product 12—and the doctors set about their research. His blood was screened for radiation. So were his feces and urine. The doctors noticed that fifteen of his teeth were decayed; they were pulled out and screened as well.

The Holy Grail of all this tissue farming was a "biochemical dosimeter," an indicator in a person's excreta that would show how much radiation he or she had received. Also on the wish list was the development of a "body-burden model," a set of statistics that would reveal how different doses of radiation affected human functioning and, ultimately, survival.

After Ebenezer's teeth had been studied, his bones and liver were next on the sampling roster—but he never gave the doctors a chance to get at them. One day a nurse opened the door to Ebenezer's room and he was gone. Perhaps he had grown suspicious of all the attention; whatever his reason, the man the doctors had written off for dead had left the hospital and moved out of state, carrying the government's plutonium with him. The physicians at Oak Ridge never saw him again.

Ebenezer's disappearance was irritating to the AEC but hardly catastrophic. By the time he fled, other doctors had already cast a wider net. Plutonium injections were under way at The Billings Hospital of the University of Chicago, and more were to follow—at the University of California Medical Center at Berkeley; Massachusetts General Hospital, Boston; Strong Memorial Hospital, Rochester, New York. The menu of injectable elements grew as well, to include zirconium, americium, and uranium. Like Ebenezer Cade, most of the people injected had no idea they had become radioactive incubators.

Who were they? Most had been diagnosed as terminally ill, although some had nothing more terminal than rheumatoid arthritis or alcoholism. Many with incurable cancers were still capable of leading active and productive lives. Nearly all were poor and indigent—charity cases who their doctors felt had no right to question or refuse any treatment they received, even if the treatment were actually a medical experiment not intended to help them and that might conceivably kill them.

Did these patients question their doctors? Not likely. People were more trusting of their physicians before it became known that their physicians might inject them with radioisotopes without asking their permission. Those who did have questions were simply told that the injection was part of their treatment.

Radiation became a favored tool among certain medical researchers, and the range of its introduction into the human body grew:

- Charity patients with incurable cancers were given large doses of Total Body Irradiation (TBI) at the University of Cincinnati Medical Center. They were told that the treatment was for their benefit—but in fact it was also part of a secret study funded by the Department of Defense to find the elusive biochemical dosimeter and to collect data on the acute effects of radiation on humans. For example: How much radiation could a person endure before he or she began to vomit? (Answer: 150–200 rad) Again, many of these patients were active despite their malignancies; several held regular jobs—until they received the TBI. Sixty of the eighty-eight people treated were dead within a year.

- Over eight hundred healthy (but poor) pregnant women at Vanderbilt University Medical Center in Nashville, Tennessee, were given a "cocktail" on their second visit to the prenatal clinic. They were not told that the cocktail contained radioactive Fe-59, in doses up to 120 milligrams, and that their unborn children had been drafted into an experimental study of iron absorption during pregnancy. Some of the radioactivity would lodge itself in the developing fetus; this, after all, was the point of the experiment. Whether it produced physical or mental defects or led to cancer will never be known, as the doctors' contemporary estimates of radiation in the newborns is now considered unreliable.

The doctors at Vanderbilt could have used another iron radioisotope, Fe-55, which was considered less hazardous. But they would have had to pay for Fe-55. They were apparently able to get Fe-59 for free.

- Seventy-four mentally retarded boys at the Walter E. Fernald State School in Waltham, Massachusetts, were fed radioactive milk to see if chemicals in breakfast cereals interfered with the intake of iron or calcium. The true nature of this experiment, funded in part by the AEC and the Quaker Oats Co., was hidden from its participants, who were told only that they were part of a nutrition study. Volunteers were promised membership in the school's "Science Club" as well as trips to the beach and a baseball game. Parents received letters explaining that boys who cooperated would receive a special diet rich in vitamins and minerals and "many additional privileges" such as "a quart of milk daily." The letters did not mention that the milk was a vehicle for radioisotopes.

Some doctors defended the M.I.T. researchers who conducted the Fernald experiment, arguing that the school provided an environment where diet could be strictly controlled. But the same control would have been available at any private boarding school near Boston. Why were the children of the privileged not recruited? Perhaps, as one researcher noted, it was unlikely that wealthy children would have volunteered in return for extra milk or a chance to go to the beach.*

• Prisoners at Oregon's state penitentiary had radioactive thymidine injected into their testicles as part of a NASA study to find out if cosmic radiation in space would make astronauts sterile. The prisoners were paid $25 an injection—and most received at least five—plus an additional $25 when they were vasectomized at the end of the experiment. (NASA wanted no genetically damaged children as a legacy of its

---

*In December 1997—forty years after the fact—M.I.T. and the Quaker Oats Co. paid $1.85 million to the families of the Fernald volunteers. In exchange, the families dropped their class-action suit in Boston's U.S. District Court. Neither the university nor the company offered apologies or admitted guilt.

study.) Accounts vary as to how many prisoners participated, but it appears to have been about a hundred. The only voice of protest was raised by the penitentiary chaplain, who forbade Roman Catholic prisoners from volunteering because they would have had to provide masturbated semen samples.

The prisoners understood that sterility was the price they would pay for their $150, but did they understand the risk of testicular infection and cancer? The doctor who injected the thymidine avoided discussing cancer with the prisoners. He explained, "I didn't want to scare them."

The fate of the Oregon prisoners remains unknown. A follow-up program designed to trace them was rejected by the state of Oregon, which cited a lack of funds.

America's radioactive human experiments ended in the early 1970s, but the cloak of secrecy surrounding them wasn't lifted until twenty years later. In January 1994 President Bill Clinton created The Advisory Committee on Human Radiation Experiments, which conducted interviews and dug through piles of formerly classified documents in an effort to unearth the truth. But as fate would have it, the committee released its findings on the same day the O.J. Simpson criminal jury delivered its verdict. Even the *New York Times* buried the radiation story on its inside pages.

One person who would have read the committee's report with interest was Ebenezer Cade. Unfortunately, he had died at the relatively early age of sixty-one, only eight years after his plutonium injection. A doctor said he died of heart failure.

# A King and a Fool

Every working man sometimes dreams of being a king. But how many are given the opportunity to become one, only to have it taken away?

Johann Augustus Sutter was a native of Switzerland, a shopkeeper by trade, a failure by habit. Beginning in Burgdorf and Basel, he was partner to a long list of business collapses that eventually got him kicked out of his house and then out of his country.

Sutter decided to seek his fortune in America, where he quickly proved just as unsuccessful. He tried first New York, then Cincinnati, then St. Louis. Investing what little he had, he became a trader on the Santa Fe Trail. He failed at that, too.

Many men would have given up. Not Johann Sutter. The grandness of the West fired his ambition. This was a place where a man was measured not by his past, but by what he could make of his future. Determined, he packed his few belongings and hit the Oregon Trail, reaching Fort Vancouver, near present-day Portland, in October 1838.

Sutter the storekeeper took measure of the land. What he saw, with his businessman's eyes, was a vast frontier with no place to shop. He dreamed of a beach-head of capitalism in this wilderness, a supply axis for immigrants to come. More than a store, more than a city, it would be the hub of its own empire, a private kingdom with Johann Sutter as its sovereign.

Sutter needed a place loosely governed and utterly iso-lated to try his grand experiment. "I preferred a country," he later explained, "where I should be absolute master." He soon learned that the most scraggly, isolated place he could hope for lay just to the south. It was called California.

California in 1838 was a sleepy Mexican province with little to suggest that it would ever be anything else. Scattered missions and forts hugged the coast from San Diego to San Francisco, a mud-flat cove where seasick sailors would stop for a night. Transportation was by horseback or ox cart.

If one trekked inland from San Francisco there was virtually nothing: no towns, no roads, only an occasional ranch. Beyond the Coast Ranges were only aboriginal people, bear, elk, wolves, coyotes. Few stayed in Califor-nia more than a day or two.

This raw land suited Sutter's plans perfectly, and he traveled to Monterey, California's provincial capital, to meet the Mexican governor. In Sutter's years of failure he had learned something of the art of salesmanship, at least as it applied to the Far West. He wore a smart, official-looking uniform and a big hat crested with feathers. He referred to himself as "Captain" Sutter. Combined with his European manners, education, and accent, he brought an air of pomp and importance to a place that had little of either.

Sutter explained that he had come to California to found a settlement for European colonists called New Helvetia (New Switzerland). When the governor asked where, exactly, he planned to settle, Sutter replied that he'd heard of a fertile central valley beyond the Coast Ranges. It would be ideal for farming, a magnet for future colonists. He would try his luck there.

The governor was pleased. This crazy European would probably get himself killed, but if he succeeded, he would be far inland and out of the way. A deal was struck: in exchange for roughly seventy-six square miles of territory and the power to act as "political authority and dispenser of justice," Sutter agreed to become a naturalized citizen of Mexico and to defend his realm from "adventurers from the United States." Just like that, Sutter had his kingship and kingdom.

From the start, New Helvetia prospered. Sutter had chosen its location wisely, at the confluence of the Sacramento and American Rivers, about eighty miles east of San Francisco. The settlement occupied one of the most strategic positions in northern California, a natural goal for immigrants following the overland trails.

What really made New Helvetia a success was Sutter's abandonment of his end of the bargain he had made. Mexico was too weak to defend its territory, and Sutter quickly shifted his practical allegiance to the United States. Rather than repel the invading Americans, he welcomed them. It didn't matter to Sutter what country his customers came from, as long as they came.

Like any prudent king, Sutter had a castle (of sorts) constructed to protect his domain. "Sutter's Fort" was a massive adobe structure covering five acres, with walls eighteen feet high and three feet thick. The battlements bristled with secondhand cannons purchased from a Russian fur company. With its living quarters, forges, shops, and granaries, Sutter's Fort became the center of trade for the entire region.

Sutter rapidly expanded the services available at New Helvetia. A blacksmith shop furnished tools, a distillery provided liquor, a launch carried freight and passengers between the settlement and San Francisco Bay. Mormons ran Sutter's tanning works, Indians tended his wheat fields, French-Canadian trappers roamed the mountains for furs and skins and tallow.

All of these acquisitions and expansions required money, and Sutter was soon deep in debt. But his skills of persuasion went far in the wilderness. "Man can fashion this place into a paradise," he preached, and the businessmen of California listened. Merchants, traders, and ship captains loaned him the supplies and tools he needed.

By 1846 Sutter owned twelve thousand head of cattle, two thousand horses and mules, more than ten thousand sheep, and a thousand hogs. His settlement boasted a ten-acre grape orchard and two acres of Castile roses. Plans were laid for a town, "Sutterville," the probable future capital of New Helvetia. War between the United States and Mexico put that project on hold, but the fighting never even came close to Sutter's Fort.

The American victory in 1848 was unsettling in only one respect: it made Sutter's land grants invalid. But that was a legal matter that would take years to resolve in the courts, if it ever got that far. Meanwhile, business was flourishing, Sutter was paying off his creditors, and he would very soon be rich. It would take a wave of unimaginable anarchy to overthrow his empire now, and with the war over and statehood assured, how could that possibly happen?

James Wilson Marshall was a thirty-six-year-old farmer and handyman who had wandered into Sutter's Fort in 1845. Like countless others, he had drifted west looking for opportunity. He was dependable and skilled, and Sutter put him to work making wheels, plows, looms, and dozens of other necessities for the fort.

If King Sutter needed a fool for his court, Marshall was a good choice. Almost everyone at the settlement pronounced him half-crazy or harebrained. He certainly had a self-centered view of the world—like Sutter—and an overwhelming confidence in his ability to do anything he put his mind to—like Sutter. Perhaps it was his attitude as much as his ability that kept Marshall on Sutter's payroll.

By the spring of 1847 New Helvetia's settlers had chopped down all the usable trees nearby, and Sutter needed lumber to build the new town. Scouting teams were sent into the mountains to find a site for a sawmill. They always returned with the same gloomy news: there was plenty of timber and water power, but no way to get the wood back to Sutter's Fort. Roads were nonexistent and the rivers upstream were whitewater, crashing through canyons that made rafting logs impossible.

James Marshall thought otherwise. He told Sutter that he would oversee construction of a sawmill at a location of his own choosing in exchange for half the lumber produced. Somehow—he never was very clear on this—he would float the wood downstream to Sutter's Fort. Sutter's advisors thought Marshall was crazy, and in hindsight, they were right. But Sutter liked Marshall's spirit. Here was a man who said yes when everyone else said no. Hadn't everyone scoffed at Sutter when he founded New Helvetia?

Sutter ignored the naysayers and agreed to Marshall's plan. Construction of the sawmill would begin immediately. Sutter figured that by the following spring it would be up, running, and turning a profit.

Marshall chose a site for the sawmill on the south fork of the American River in the Coloma Valley, about fifty miles upstream from Sutter's Fort. Beginning in September, working through the fall and into winter, Marshall and his crew cleared the land and built the mill. It was a life without many comforts; even the water from the river tasted bad. The cook, who'd worked in South American goldfields, said that its heavy sediment reminded him of gold-bearing ore. That gave the crew a good chuckle. No one bothered to check it out.

By late January the work was nearly complete. All that remained was to widen the millrace to increase flow to the waterwheel. Marshall ordered some digging and blasting, then the crew turned in for the night. The rushing river water would scour away the leftover sand and gravel while they slept.

At 7:30 the next morning, January 19, 1848, Marshall inspected the millrace. He looked down into the icy water and there, six inches beneath the surface, was a gold nugget. It was worth at the time maybe fifty cents. Marshall lifted it out of the water and stared at it long and hard. Gold in the American River? Impossible. He looked again and saw another nugget, and another, and another, and another. He picked one up and hit it with a rock. It flattened but it didn't break—just like pure gold.

Marshall ran to tell the crew, but they didn't believe crazy James Marshall. He had the cook boil a nugget in lye to bring out its color, then he hammered it into a thin foil. Now the crew believed him. The next morning, Marshall grabbed more nuggets from the millrace, mounted his horse, and rode hellbent-for-leather to Sutter's Fort.

Marshall could barely contain his excitement when he showed the nuggets to Sutter. They were millionaires! Sutter saw the picture more clearly—and was horrified. The last thing New Helvetia needed right now was an attack of gold fever. Maybe in a year, maybe even in six months, but not *now*. Sutter's kingdom was still unfinished and very vulnerable.

Sutter decided to take a look for himself. Perhaps Marshall's find was just a fluke. Maybe there was only a little gold. . . .

A day at the mill dashed those hopes. Gold was everywhere; you could scrape it out of the ground with a pocketknife. Marshall's crew, whose work had slowed considerably in his absence, had clawed ten times its weekly salary in one day from the hills and streams around the mill. It was an omen of things to come. Sutter knew it.

Sutter swore the men to secrecy, then considered his options. He couldn't throw prospectors off his land; New Helvetia was only "his" in the courts of Mexico, and Mexico no longer owned California. If he could keep the story quiet, he could finish the lumber and flour mills. Then he could supply prospectors—if there weren't too many— with provisions. He could maintain control of the land.

Events, however, were already spinning out of Sutter's control. Back at the fort, one of Marshall's men walked into the general store and bought a bottle of brandy. He paid for it with a gold nugget. When the clerk asked where it came from, the secret was out.

Sutter's men began to disappear from New Helvetia, gradually at first. A blacksmith here, a weaver there; he could do nothing to stop them. Sutter paid his workers $1.25 a day, but the men in the goldfields could pocket $50 in an afternoon. It was so easy.

Still, Sutter hoped the fever would pass. He hadn't figured on Sam Brannan. Brannan owned the general store at Sutter's Fort, and he also published a newspaper in San Francisco. When the clerk got word downriver about the gold, Brannan ran a story on it. The people of San Francisco, skeptical and not particularly literate, ignored the news. But Brannan was intrigued. He took a boat up to Sutter's Fort and watched as the first prospectors returned from the foothills, their pockets filled with gold dust and nuggets.

Being a Mormon elder, Brannan immediately demanded a 30 percent "tithe" in gold from every Mormon in the group. (He claimed it was for construction of a temple, but nearly all of it stayed in his pocket.) He then returned to San Francisco, bought all the pans, picks, and shovels in town, and sent them back upriver on the first boat he could find— with orders to his clerk to jack up the prices. Then he poured his gold dust into a bottle, raised it over his head, and rode up and down the streets of San Francisco screaming, "Gold! Gold from the American River!!!" This time, the people listened.

San Francisco was half empty within three weeks. Schoolteachers, carpenters, and cooks left their jobs and headed for Sutter's Fort. Farmers deserted their fields, sailors abandoned their ships, Sam Brannan's newspaper folded for a lack of staff.

Seeing the rush, Sutter's remaining workers dropped their tools and fled to the millsite, hoping to strike it rich. Tanners, lumberjacks, stockmen—everybody left. Sutter's eighteen-foot-high, three-foot-thick walls could not stop the exodus.

By mid-summer the people of San Jose, Monterey, Santa Barbara, Los Angeles, and San Diego were heading for the foothills. By autumn two-thirds of Oregon's men had trekked south. And by the following summer the forty-niners had come, pouring into California from the eastern seaboard, Europe, Central America, South America, Asia, and the Pacific Islands. All of them were bound for the new El Dorado that had, until very recently, been the property of Johann Sutter.

If Sutter thought the rich and powerful would rally to his side, he quickly learned otherwise. An appeal to Washington brought no relief. The federal government refused to even acknowledge, let alone assist, the former Mexican titleholder to the biggest mineral bonanza in United States history. It wanted as many people as possible in California, digging up gold.

Within a year of Marshall's discovery, thousands of prospectors had created a tent city at Sutter's Fort. Miners overran the settlement, staking, claiming, and taking every piece of land. They trampled Sutter's crops, butchered his livestock, ran off with his tools and supplies. "There is a saying that men will steal everything but a milestone and a millstone," Sutter wrote. "They stole my millstones."

Dismembered by trappers, lawyers, soldiers, and people from nearly every other occupation who wanted to strike it rich, New Helvetia had ceased to exist. Unable to pay his debts, Sutter went bankrupt in 1852.

Disgusted, he moved north with his family—where rustlers again stole his cattle and squatters again overran his property. Vigilantes set fire to his house and destroyed it. Sutter packed what little of his property remained and moved to Pennsylvania.

Meanwhile, James Marshall had tried to make a living from the sawmill he had built. After cutting a few thousand feet of lumber he gave up; like Sutter, he couldn't hold onto his men. The millsite was soon overrun by squatters and Marshall abandoned it, helpless to defend the property. He became just another prospector.

Other miners dogged him, convinced that he had a magic touch, even threatening to hang him if he didn't find more gold. Marshall never could. He gradually sank into alcoholism and madness, convinced that he owned all the gold in California. The other prospectors drove him from the goldfields. Perhaps Marshall could have made a fresh start in San Francisco, but the steamers that churned the river now charged $30 a trip. Marshall couldn't afford the fare.

Meanwhile, the man most responsible for Sutter and Marshall's woes, Sam Brannan, had continued to resell supplies and food to miners at extortionate prices. He was now California's first millionaire. The Mormon church expelled him, but if that bothered Brannan, it didn't show. He went on to become a San Francisco banker, a powerful landowner, a senator in the state legislature, and a companion of European courtesan Lola Montez.

By the end of the Civil War, $785 million in gold—roughly $19 billion today—had been ripped out of the foothills and streams of California. California gold had financed two

American wars, removed the unskilled (and unwanted) from crowded eastern cities, filled banks, boosted prices and wages, fattened the rich, and made America's politicians and military leaders look like geniuses.

Marshall and Sutter, however, were both nearly broke. They bitterly resented their misfortune; Sutter especially, whose empire had been destroyed and who now read his name in history books, forever associated with riches and glory that he had never enjoyed.

In 1880 seventy-seven-year-old Johann Sutter journeyed to Washington to seek compensation for his losses. The Senate considered a bill that would grant Sutter a one-time payment of $50,000. Rather than act, it adjourned for its summer recess. Two days later Sutter died, broken and beaten.

Marshall was still alive—barely. In answer to his pleas, California had awarded him a pension of $100 a month, to be reassessed every two years. When Marshall went to the state capital of Sacramento—the city that had been built instead of Sutterville—to ask for an extension, a brandy bottle fell from his pocket and rolled along the floor of the state assembly. Offended by this breach of decorum, the well-to-do senators cut him off without a penny.

Marshall quickly sank into self-imposed isolation, a sick man living in a Spartan homesteader's cabin, feeding himself from a subsistence garden. He died there in 1885, alone and insignificant.

James Marshall's $200 estate did not include the gold nugget he had found at Sutter's sawmill years earlier. He had mistakenly spent it on food.

# A Matter of Trust

THE BROCHURE COPY READ, "NATHAN STUBBLEFIELD WIRE-less Telephone. May be placed in your office, parlor, flying car, auto, airship, water craft or other vehicle. This invention is the triumph of the age, and is worth A SHIPLOAD OF GOLD."

The brochure was printed in 1908.

If it throws your sense of history and technology out of kilter to read a wireless phone ad from 1908, you're not alone. What's more, this remarkable device was invented by a self-taught melon farmer from rural Kentucky. And it wasn't even his greatest creation.

Nathan Stubblefield was born, lived, and died in Calloway County, just north of the Kentucky-Tennessee line. He raised gourds and apples on a few scrappy acres near the village of Murray, living in a modest house with his wife and nine children.

When Nathan was born in the summer of 1859, nothing suggested that he would be anything different from or better than his neighbors or siblings. The Stubblefields were solvent, steady people.

But Nathan was unusual. He had few friends. Even when he was a child, folks around Murray called him "peculiar" and "queer" and left him alone. That was all right with Nathan. His self-imposed isolation gave him more time to devote to his life's passion: electricity. He left school at fifteen and read everything he could about the experiments of Michael Faraday, Joseph Henry, and Thomas Edison. He would disappear from the farm to spend hours in the offices of the local newspaper, the only place in Calloway County that had copies of *Scientific American*.

Stubblefield wanted to be a world-renowned inventor, and he wanted to be rich. And he was going to use electricity to make it happen.

In 1882, confident that he was onto something, he staged a demonstration for his neighbors. He wired together some batteries and fed their electric current into the ground. Several yards away, a compass needle began to spin wildly. See?, Stubblefield said. If the earth could carry electromagnetic effects, why couldn't it carry power? Or a telegraph signal? The people of Murray stifled a collective yawn. What did this have to do with farming? Angry and frustrated, Stubblefield stomped back to his house and slammed the door. Next time he'd show them something they'd never forget.

It was at about this time that Nathan Stubblefield developed an intense distrust of other human beings. Everyone was a potential thief of his inventions: neighbors, friends, even his own wife and children. He set up a tiny laboratory on the front porch of his house and refused to allow anyone inside or to let any member of his family leave the farm without him. The Stubblefield children were taken out of school and educated at home. Nathan Stubblefield's reputation grew, not as a genius but as an eccentric.

In 1892 Stubblefield invited a young attorney named Rainey Wells over to the farm (but not inside the house) and handed him a small keg with a telephone earpiece on top. Stubblefield told him to walk to a spot several hundred yards inside the apple orchard. Rainey later recalled, "I had hardly reached my post...when I heard 'Hello Rainey!' come booming out of the receiver. I jumped a foot...but there were no wires, I tell you."

Using a haphazard collection of farm hardware and secondhand junk, Stubblefield had somehow invented an electromagnetic induction telephone. He created an electromagnetic field by feeding current into a large loop of wire that he had strung in his apple trees. When Rainey walked into this field, it induced current in a second, smaller loop of wire inside the keg. This current created an electrical connection between the two loops—without connecting wires—that carried Stubblefield's voice from his mouthpiece in the house to Rainey's earpiece on the keg.

Electromagnetic induction was nothing new. Stubblefield had probably read about it in one of his prized copies of *Electrical World* magazine. But what he did with it was completely new: sending and receiving the human voice without wires.

In the following years, Stubblefield would talk, count numbers, whistle, whisper, and play the harmonica from the house while selected neighbors stared at the keg in amazement. Their astonishment is understandable; this was, after all, Calloway County, not the Edison Laboratory. To put Stubblefield's accomplishment in perspective, the first transmission of the human voice by radio—what most histories incorrectly cite as the first transmission of the human voice, period—wasn't made until Christmas Eve 1906, fourteen years after Rainey Wells stood in Nathan Stubblefield's apple orchard.

Stubblefield wasn't satisfied. Long-distance voice transmission required larger wire loops and more current than he could produce. He never could get this first phone to work at a distance greater than a half mile. But "Crazy Nate" kept at it, laboring in secrecy, handicapped by a lack of funds, equipment, and contact with other researchers. His suspicions of others deepened. He had his home wired so that strangers approaching within a half mile would set off a battery of bells. Unwanted visitors would be waved away by a shotgun.

Nathan Stubblefield would perhaps have spent his whole life this way, shut off from the world, never satisfied that his invention was good enough. But in mid-December 1901, Guglielmo Marconi successfully transmitted the telegraph letter "s" by wireless across the Atlantic. The press went wild. Marconi was hailed as a genius and the father of a new science that would transform the world.

Stubblefield fumed. The letter "s" in Morse code was three simple dots; Stubblefield had transmitted the human voice! Too envious to keep quiet any longer, he told the people of Murray that on New Year's Day 1902 he would unveil his invention to the world. It would, he hinted, put Marconi's accomplishment on the back page where it belonged.

Stubblefield's reputation among the locals had grown considerably since 1882. A thousand people turned out on the courthouse square that freezing January morning, perhaps in anticipation of getting a good laugh out of the county kook.

If that was their expectation, Nathan Stubblefield disappointed them. The invention he unveiled was not the one that had dazzled Rainey Wells ten years earlier. This one was significantly better.

The keg had been replaced by five mysterious black boxes, each roughly two feet square. A sixth, larger box resembling a speaker's lectern served as Nathan's broadcasting station. Bolted into the top of each box was a modified candlestick telephone, connected to the interior by a wire. More wire coiled out of the left and right sides of each box, their ends wrapped around two-foot-long steel rods.

Stubblefield set up his transmitter on the square and invited any five onlookers to each take a box, go anywhere they wanted, plunge the rods into the ground, and listen. When they did, they were amazed. Stubblefield's voice and ever-present harmonica music poured out of the receivers, clear and strong. It was the first wireless broadcast of the human voice in history.

Nathan Stubblefield was using the natural conduction transmission method he'd explored twenty years earlier. It required no loop of wire, and the receiver didn't have to be in a particular spot. Instead, the voice-carrying current was transmitted through the earth. The rods tethered to the boxes acted as receiving antennae. But, again, it was *what* they received that was so remarkable—the human voice, sent through the earth without wires.

Word of Nathan Stubblefield's impossible invention sped to nearby cities: Memphis, St. Louis, Nashville. The *St. Louis Post-Dispatch* sent a reporter to investigate. Stubblefield explained that what Marconi had done was good, but what he had done was much, much better. "I have solved the problem of telephoning without wires through the earth, as Signor Marconi has of sending signals through space," he told the *Post-Dispatch*. With a little more time, he predicted, his invention could be improved "until messages by voice can be sent and heard all over the country, to Europe, all over the world."

"There is nothing to stop it," he said. "The world is its limit."

Stubblefield let the reporter roam the farm for an hour, thrusting the rods into the ground wherever he wished, listening to Stubblefield's son Bernard talk and play music. Even a mile away the sound was clear. The reporter was impressed. The paper ran the story big. People outside of Kentucky began to take an interest in Nathan Stubblefield.

Stubblefield had picked a good time to unveil his creation. The stock market was booming in 1902. Investors and speculators who had watched with envy as the telephone made its backers wealthy were looking for sexy new technologies. Marconi's success only increased their hunger. If they could back a winner early, they could become very rich.

Scientists and capitalists "wearing diamonds as large as your thumb" came to Murray to court the mysterious inventor. Most of them were turned away with the barrel of Stubblefield's shotgun. He reportedly rejected a written offer of $40,000 for a partial interest in his wireless phone. He desperately needed the money, but he felt the offer asked too much for too little.

Friends urged him to patent his invention for the protection it would provide. Stubblefield refused. The wireless telephone wasn't perfect yet; it needed an amplifier to increase its range and a frequency tuner to lock out wayward signals. These improvements required outside capital. But the thought of sharing his glory with anyone else, even through a business arrangement, was intolerable to Nathan Stubblefield. Always lurking in his paranoid mind was the fear that a slick operator would rip him off.

Finally, his need for money overpowered his caution. Stubblefield gave in. In exchange for all rights to the ground conduction telephone, a group of Manhattan investors would incorporate the Wireless Telephone Company of America, capitalize it for $5 million, and give Stubblefield five hundred thousand shares at a dollar apiece. The company would then develop franchises for the invention and provide Stubblefield with the resources necessary to perfect it.

His neighbors and long-suffering family were jubilant. At last Nathan had learned that through cooperation there would come progress, financial rewards, and the promise of more riches to come. The deal with the Manhattan investors was a brave gesture of trust for this socially fragile, pathologically suspicious man.

Its betrayal would send him over the edge into madness.

In the beginning, things went well. The backers asked Stubblefield to take the phone on tour to promote the sale of stock, which must have soothed his battered ego. These new demonstrations would not be given in backwoods Kentucky—Nathan would travel to where the money was: Washington, D.C., Philadelphia, and New York.

Philadelphia and Washington were triumphs. In Philadelphia, Stubblefield took his wireless phone out to Fairmount Park before a critical audience of inventors, statesmen, businessmen, and newspaper reporters and transmitted voice and music to them from a house a mile away. The demonstration in Washington was even more spectacular. For four hours Stubblefield broadcast to shorebound scientists and journalists from a boat cruising on the Potomac River.

The Washington demonstration also gave Stubblefield a revealing view of his business partners' priorities. Stubblefield later claimed that while he was setting up his telephone, one of the company directors asked him to rig a secret buried wire between the transmitter and receiver for a land demonstration. "They said they could sell more stock that way," he recalled. "I wouldn't do it."

Still, the journalists and promoters were pleased, and the scientists were stumped. Everyone admitted that this melon farmer from rural Kentucky had created something new and extraordinary. Nathan Stubblefield was hailed as the inventor of the wireless telephone in newspapers all along the East Coast.

Then came New York. It was a disaster. The background noise from Manhattan's maze of underground telephone and power lines rendered Stubblefield's invention useless. Apparently no one had considered that not every patch of ground was as tranquil as the earth of Calloway County.

A frequency tuner—one of the improvements that Stubblefield wanted to make—would have solved the problem. But the directors of the Wireless Telephone Company of America weren't interested in making improvements. They were interested in selling stock, pocketing the money, and getting out. Perhaps they believed that Stubblefield's phone would require too much capital to make it profitable. Or perhaps they were, as Stubblefield always asserted, "damned rascals" who intended stock fraud from the very beginning.

After six months of glory, it was all over. Nathan Stubblefield had lost control of his invention. His friends and supporters in Murray had lost their investments. Stubblefield never got a dime for his five hundred thousand shares. "There remains nothing for me to do," he wrote the company secretary, "but go home." And he did.

Nathan Stubblefield did make one last stab at success, the 1908 "shipload of gold" portable phone. It was an applied version of his induction system, with an O-shaped antenna as big as a car tire attached to a candlestick phone (this replaced the wire coil in the keg). Unfortunately, the system would have required that elevated wires be strung along both sides of every road on which it would be used. It was wildly impractical. It bombed.

Cheated of his fame and fortune, more bitter and suspicious than ever, Stubblefield became impossible to live with. After years of funneling every penny into his experiments, he lost the farm. His wife and children abandoned him, though it could be argued that he'd abandoned them years earlier.

Nathan Stubblefield could have fought back. He could have taken the New York investors to court, and he might have won. With some capital he could have reduced the size of his phones or increased their range or made them tunable. Any one of these improvements would have made them commercially attractive. Soldiers or explorers or people living in remote areas could have used them. They could have served as a forerunner to today's highway emergency phones. He could have marketed them as toys for children.

But Nathan Stubblefield was through with the outside world. People had betrayed him, as he always knew they would. He moved to the farm of a sympathetic neighbor, where he built a crude one-room hut out of scrap lumber and tin, which he lined with cornstalks to keep out the wind. From this hovel he continued his experiments alone, year after year. Neighbors spoke of lights appearing in trees, on the ends of steel rods, and along a wire fence. Voices, apparently from the air, barked at trespassers.

In March of 1928, Stubblefield dropped out of sight completely. Two weeks later the county coroner kicked in Stubblefield's front door and found the inventor of the wireless telephone dead of malnutrition. Strewn about were Stubblefield's beloved copies of *Electrical World*, now rotted with age. Scraps of metal and wire littered the floor. Stubblefield had apparently destroyed all of his prototypes.

Nathan Stubblefield's secrets died with him on the dirt floor of that tin-roofed shack. The man who could see so far into the future reportedly had his eyes eaten by a half-starved cat.

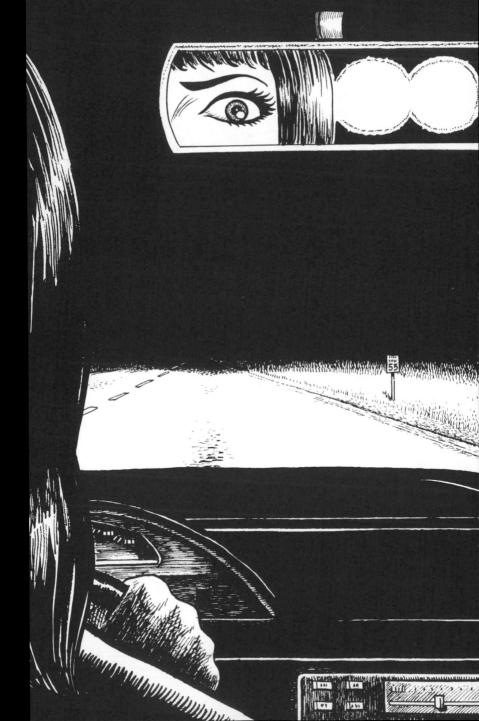

# 10

# Whistleblower

AMERICA'S ANTINUCLEAR MOVEMENT HAS FADED IN RECENT years to a historical curiosity, a dated relic usually dismissed with a collective shrug. Yet those who recall the chant of "No more nukes!" also recall the movement's hero, Karen Silkwood, who never lived to enjoy her popularity. Few individuals in the twentieth century have been screwed in so many nasty ways by so many powerful groups for so foul a purpose.

Karen Silkwood came from Texas, where with straight A's and fondness for chemistry, she had earned a degree in medical technology. She was bright, young, and in search of a job in which she could use her skills. In 1972 the Kerr-McGee Nuclear Corporation hired her as a laboratory analyst at their plant on the Cimarron River, six miles south of Crescent, Oklahoma.

Kerr-McGee was a subcontractor for the Atomic Energy Commission (AEC). Its workers in the Cimarron

River plant processed plutonium into pellets, then loaded them into eight-foot-long stainless-steel fuel rods. Kerr-McGee had a fixed-fee contract of $7.2 million from the AEC to produce over sixteen thousand rods, which would power an experimental "fast-breeder" reactor that the AEC wanted to build in Tennessee. The fixed-fee condition of the contract meant the more money Kerr-McGee could save in production, the more Kerr-McGee would profit.

This arrangement worked well until the spring of 1974. By then the AEC was in trouble. Their fast-breeder program was $800 million over budget and Congress was dangerously close to finding that out. The AEC wanted fuel rods and it wanted them quick. That was fine with Kerr-McGee; more rods in less time meant more profit for the corporation. The workers in the Cimarron River plant—mostly poor, uneducated Oklahomans—would have to step up production, but Kerr-McGee was not particularly concerned about them or the fitness of the product they were producing.

Into this morass walked Karen Silkwood, whose job was to perform quality-control tests on Kerr-McGee pellets and rods and reject those that she found defective. She carried some heavy personal baggage in her ninety-eight-pound frame. Silkwood drank, smoked pot, popped Quaaludes when she felt she needed to, had abandoned three children by a previous marriage, had once attempted suicide, and may have been bisexual. At twenty-eight she was far from scandal free, which is to say that she was little more than modern and human. She also possessed a lockjawed sense of right and wrong. What she saw at Kerr-McGee set her teeth on edge.

The workers in the Cimarron River plant toiled seven days a week in twelve-hour shifts. While college-educated Silkwood peered into microscopes in the metallography lab, high-school dropouts mixed, baked, and loaded Kerr-McGee's plutonium in production rooms. These were cesspools of rotting gaskets, broken respirators, and equipment that was cleaned with contaminated towels. Plutonium spills and leaks were common; workers were splashed with radiation, breathed radiation, ingested radiation. Those who complained too loudly were fired, and jobs were hard to find in central Oklahoma in 1974. The people around Crescent were grateful to labor in Kerr-McGee's plant for three dollars an hour.

By August 1974, Silkwood had seen enough. Alarmed by what was going on around her, she became a member of her union's bargaining committee. The committee's immediate—and apparently hopeless—task was to convince the Cimarron River plant work force that their union was more valuable than the 10-percent wage increase Kerr-McGee promised if the workers would kick the union out. Silkwood's assignment was health and safety.

She had never been an activist. In any other job, for any other employer, she probably would have led a relatively uneventful life. But Kerr-McGee was no ordinary boss and the plutonium plant on the Cimarron River was no nine-to-five office.

In her role as health and safety committeewoman, Silkwood began exploring the plant, documenting safety violations and interviewing the workers. The stories she recorded were startling. Plutonium dust was tracked through the plant, and sometimes out into town, by unknowing employees. Workers were ordered to ignore emergency alarms and to work in contaminated rooms. Security was a joke. Farm kids were purposely kept ignorant of the dangerous substances that they routinely touched and breathed.

By late September Silkwood had gathered enough material to merit a trip to the union's legislative office in Washington, D.C. Two pieces of important information surfaced at that meeting. First, Silkwood learned from the union officers that plutonium was carcinogenic. In retrospect her ignorance seems astonishing, but Karen Silkwood was no dummy. In 1974 such information was hidden from the public. Airborne plutonium dust at the Cimarron River plant lodged in workers' lungs, spilled plutonium solution reached their blood through cuts in the skin, plutonium nitrate mist eventually found its way into their livers and bones. In twenty years Silkwood and her co-workers could be riddled with malignant tumors, and Kerr-McGee hadn't told a soul.

Second, the union officers learned from Silkwood that Kerr-McGee was tampering with quality-control records. This revelation was a godsend to the union, which was looking for dramatic allegations to use to secure a favorable bargaining position. The deliberate shipping of defective fuel rods, which could possibly lead to a nuclear explosion, was incredible news. The union decided not to tell the AEC, which they regarded as a group of untrustworthy bootlickers. Instead, Silkwood's information would go directly to the *New York Times*—if she could get documents to confirm it. "If we can prove that," the union officers told Silkwood, "we can get Kerr-McGee up against the wall with publicity."

Karen Silkwood, who only two months earlier had been just another faceless employee, suddenly found herself a corporate spy with the health of her co-workers riding on her shoulders. Her opponent was a Fortune 500 company with many powerful friends in Oklahoma. As it turned out, Kerr McGee had other, even more powerful friends lurking in the shadows. But Silkwood was unaware of that in September 1974, and she gamely agreed to go forward with the plan.

Silkwood spent the last six weeks of her life poring over records in the metallography lab. She found dozens of falsified quality-control reports as well as doctored photographs of fuel rods that had been retouched to cover cracks and other defects. She was a painfully obvious spy. Her position in the union had already made her a target of management scrutiny, and her wandering around the plant, talking to workers and jotting down notes, and after-shift interest in safety and quality-control records made it easy to guess what she was up to. Everyone at the plant knew.

If Silkwood was willing to stick her neck out, Kerr-McGee was more than willing to chop it in two. The company, it later became clear, recruited members of Oklahoma City's police intelligence unit to tap Silkwood's phone, bug her apartment, and break into her car—criminal activity that violated both federal and state laws. Kerr-McGee apparently secured police cooperation by telling them that Karen Silkwood was an antinuclear activist (in those days also known as "dissidents," "left-wingers," and "subversives") as well as a suspected member of a pluto-nium smuggling ring. Pot-smoking, Quaalude-popping, sexually liberated Karen Silkwood had a personality that would easily arouse the suspicion and ire of a 1974 law enforcement officer.

Perhaps Kerr-McGee actually believed that Silkwood was a plutonium smuggler. More likely, it cynically fabri-cated this suspicion to get the police to monitor her activities.

Plutonium smuggling at the Cimarron River plant was one of many fuzzy edges to the Silkwood story. Kerr-McGee had known since 1973 that plutonium was disap-pearing from its inventory. In the beginning the company reported it to the AEC, which ordered the plant shut down until all of the plutonium could be accounted for. Then, suddenly, the AEC reversed itself and told Kerr-McGee that it could reopen the plant; in fact, it gave Kerr-McGee permission to lose even more plutonium before it was required to contact the AEC again. This was very odd behavior from a supposed regulatory agency, even one as easygoing as the AEC. Several pounds of plutonium, if it had been dumped in a pile and hidden somewhere, could reach critical mass and cause a nuclear explosion. Why was the AEC being so casual?

Apparently the AEC had been ordered to drop its investigation. The missing plutonium was no longer in the Cimarron River plant anyway. It had been smuggled past the plant's laughable security and more would fol-low, a little at a time, in a steady stream. Karen Silkwood stumbled upon this dirty secret while hunting for quality-control violations. By then the amount of missing pluto-nium totaled forty pounds, a frightful amount to lose, even in a plant as hellishly sloppy as Kerr-McGee's. Forty pounds of plutonium is enough to build three nuclear warheads.

As clichéd as it may sound today, Kerr-McGee's plutonium thief was evidently the CIA, which at the time was diverting nuclear material from several American plants to "friendly" nations as a way of evading anti-nuclear proliferation agreements. (The forty pounds from the Cimarron River plant reportedly went to Israel.) Stealing plutonium was, of course, completely illegal, and a number of powerful people would be seriously inconvenienced if the activity became known. It's possible that Karen Silkwood had documents concerning the missing plutonium with her on the night she died. If so, she was blind to the extreme measures some would be willing to take to get them back.

Silkwood may have been brash, independent, stubborn, and passionate about "kicking ass" at Kerr-McGee, but she was not shatterproof. The union was pressuring her to deliver damaging evidence. Kerr-McGee and her family were pressuring her to quit. She was pressuring herself not to. She told her friends that she was scared of the plant and that she wanted to leave but not until her job was finished. The workers needed her. Kerr-McGee had to be brought down.

Three times in three days, from November 5 to 7, Karen Silkwood was tested and found to be contaminated with plutonium. At first the contamination was determined to have come from what appeared to be a deliberate "salting" of her workplace in the plant. Then her apartment was tested and found peppered with radioactive pollution. Most perplexing of all, the strongest readings came from her toilet seat and her refrigerator, which were two hundred and eight hundred times more contaminated than the levels considered safe by even the lax standards of the AEC. No one could figure out how the plutonium got onto Silkwood and into her apartment.

Kerr-McGee later proclaimed that Silkwood had deliberately dosed herself to embarrass the company. The AEC disagreed but couldn't (or wouldn't) name who it thought was responsible. Karen Silkwood had her own theory: the contamination was coming back out of her own body.*

By now, Silkwood was scared to death and convinced that someone was trying to kill her. It didn't help to see her possessions sealed in fifty-five-gallon drums by people wearing radiation-protective suits. Nor did it help to have an attorney from Kerr-McGee corner her in her car and try to force a statement from her absolving the company of all responsibility for her health problems. It was all part of the show, Karen's friends would later conclude, part of Kerr-McGee's plan of harassment designed to push Karen Silkwood over the edge and out of the Cimarron River plant. Her ex-boyfriend remembered, "She was crying and shaking like a leaf. She kept saying she was going to die. I'd never seen her so scared."

Karen Silkwood was falling apart at the seams. Terror will do that to a person. But whoever was harassing her

---

*Karen Silkwood's autopsy showed that she had, in fact, ingested plutonium within thirty days of her death. Where and how no one could say.

underestimated Silkwood's sense of moral obligation, which kept her going long after animal fear told her to quit and get out.

At 6 P.M. on November 13, 1974, Karen Silkwood attended a union meeting at the Hub Café in Crescent. Though no one else there knew it, she had a scheduled rendezvous in two hours in Oklahoma City with a reporter for the *New York Times*. It was there that she planned to give the *Times* the documents she had been collecting for the past six weeks.

One of the union members noticed that Karen was carrying a large brown folder thick with papers and what appeared to be photographs. In the folder, Silkwood confided just before she left, was proof that Kerr-McGee had falsified quality-control records.

Karen Silkwood left the café at 7:15, driving south on Highway 74, an arrow-straight, rural two-lane blacktop that passed the Cimarron River plant. Thirty miles away lay Oklahoma City. She never made it. A truck driver heading north found her car about a half hour later, just off the road, crumpled in the entrance of a concrete culvert that passed beneath the highway. Karen Silkwood was dead of multiple and compound fractures.

The Oklahoma Highway Patrol quickly declared that Karen Silkwood had, in effect, killed herself. She was exhausted, she had been drinking, she was sedated on drugs, and she fell asleep behind the wheel, drifted off the road, crashed, and died. Later investigations blew holes in every one of those assertions and revealed that an anonymous source had provided the patrol with disinformation. A wealth of evidence surfaced that painted a dramatically different picture.

In the opinion of investigators not associated with the Oklahoma Highway Patrol (including the FBI), the last minutes of Karen Silkwood's life unfolded this way: When Silkwood left the Hub Café she had apparently been followed. Seven miles south of town and about a mile past the Cimarron River plant, where Highway 74 becomes rural and deserted, a car bumped Silkwood's from behind, carjacking style, and then tried to cut her off.

In an evasive maneuver—Karen was a trophy-winning autocross racer, and her Honda Civic was outfitted for performance driving—Silkwood drove along the banked grass shoulder for nearly 250 feet in an attempt to outflank the pursuing car. Since the road was straight and had no guardrails, her attention was focused on the car driving parallel to hers, keeping her off the asphalt. She apparently never saw the shoulder drop away from under her, replaced by the open-air entrance to a culvert. The Civic flew into the 24-foot-wide gap. Its speed wasn't enough to clear it. The car traveled forward and downward, smashed into the concrete retaining wall on the far side, and slid into the culvert entrance. Her pursuers, apparently frightened by this unexpected turn of events, sped away without retrieving the documents they had been after.

That proved not to be a problem. When Karen Silkwood's friends and the *Times* reporter found the garage where her car had been towed, the brown folder with the Kerr-McGee evidence was gone. According to the garage owner, the papers had been in the car when it arrived. Several hours later, two separate groups wearing radiation-protective suits, one claiming to be from Kerr-McGee and one claiming to be from the AEC, visited the wrecked car. They said that they had come to check for possible contamination, but they also paid a great deal of attention to the papers. After they left, Karen Silkwood's documents were gone. They remain missing to this day.

Eight days after Karen Silkwood's death, the Justice Department ordered the FBI to investigate the case. Exactly what they were looking for and what they found, no one would say, although it later became evident that they'd discovered Kerr-McGee's harassment of Silkwood and that they knew Silkwood's death was no accident. It was also apparent that they worked with Kerr-McGee to keep the messy truth hidden, helping the company to torpedo a congressional investigation and posthumously slander Silkwood as a vindictive, mentally unstable drug addict. Why they went to such trouble has never been explained. The FBI investigation was closed, quietly, five and a half months later.* Its findings were never released.

Kerr-McGee and the FBI never faced justice for covering up Karen Silkwood's murder. The judge presiding

---

*In August 1975 a representative from the National Organization for Women met with Justice Department officials and urged them to reopen the investigation. They told her that Karen Silkwood might have been a "kook" and suggested that the reason NOW members had raised concerns about the unsolved aspects of the case was because they "watched too much television."

over her negligence trial dismissed the conspiracy charges against them, ruling that the events surrounding her death were not relevant to the case.

After eleven weeks of sworn testimony, an Oklahoma City jury found Kerr-McGee responsible for the contamination in Karen Silkwood's apartment and awarded her family $10.5 million in damages. Kerr-McGee doggedly dragged the settlement through court battles for the next seven years, hoping to exhaust the funds and patience of the Silkwood family. The jury award was reduced to $5,000 by the Federal Court of Appeals, an amount covering only the personal property lost during the cleanup of Karen Silkwood's apartment. Finally, in 1986, twelve years after Silkwood's death, the suit was headed for a retrial when it was settled out of court for $1.3 million.

Those who might have pursued the Silkwood case further—women's advocates, antinuclear activists, the labor movement—apparently felt that they'd squeezed as much justice from it as could reasonably be expected. Kerr-McGee's parent company closed the Cimarron River plant in 1975 and redirected its business toward fossil fuels, where it remains an industry player today. President Jimmy Carter disbanded the AEC in 1977 and replaced it with the Department of Energy. The FBI and CIA remain aloof, their files sealed from public scrutiny.

In death, Karen Silkwood has served many masters. Hollywood turned her story into a profitable film. Two best sellers championed her cause and proclaimed victory for her principles. *Rolling Stone* ran numerous articles about her case and boosted its circulation and advertising rates.

Karen Silkwood, of course, was not around to share in the general good karma: she had died years before, alone and terrified, on a dark Oklahoma road. The documents that she gave her life to collect never reached daylight. Perhaps they, like Silkwood herself and the messy wad of loose ends that she embodied, are buried in an obscure grave, slowly turning to dust. For some still-interested parties, it can't happen fast enough.

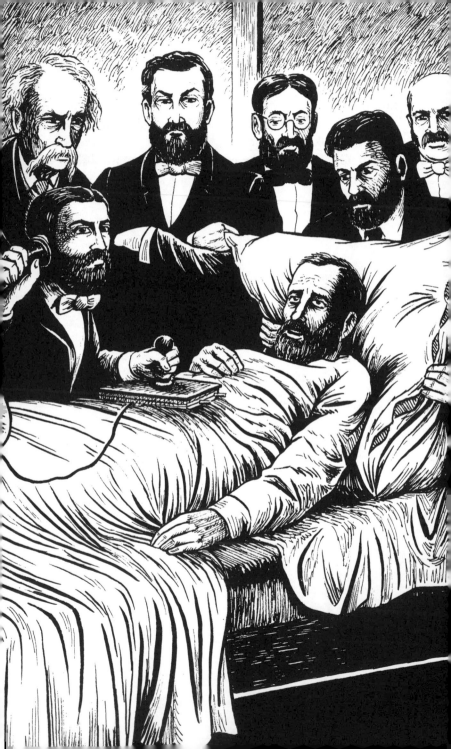

# 11

# The Unluckiest President

THE REPUBLICAN CONVENTION WAS DEADLOCKED. IT WAS June 1880, and Rutherford B. Hayes, the incumbent president, had decided not to seek a second term. Half of the party (the "Stalwarts") wanted Ulysses S. Grant, the former chief executive, to run again. The other half (the "Half-breeds") wanted to nominate James Blaine, a senator and the leader of their faction. Neither side would budge.

Finally, six days into the convention, on the thirty-sixth ballot, the Half-breeds suggested one of their own as a compromise: James Abram Garfield, who was only at the convention because he had just been elected a senator from Ohio. The Stalwarts agreed to the bargain, but only if one of their loyal men, Chester Arthur, was made Garfield's running mate.

Who was James Abram Garfield? Born dirt-poor on an Ohio farm, he had been a teacher, minister, lawyer, a general in the Union Army, and finally a member of the U.S. House of Representatives. He was one of the last members of Congress to be born in a log cabin and the first to have a telephone in his office. What perhaps appealed most to the Stalwarts was that he was neither forceful nor assertive. He drifted with the times, a firm believer in playing by the rules and following orders. The voters liked him not for what he promised, but for where he'd come from. They saw him as living proof that diligent effort brought worldly success in America.

Garfield mounted an undistinguished five-month campaign, pledging to ban Chinese immigration and support civil-service reform. He won the election by a mere seven thousand votes, less than 0.1 percent of the total ballots cast, and on March 4, 1881, James Abram Garfield was sworn in as the twentieth president of the United States. At age forty-nine he was the third-youngest man ever to hold that office.

Garfield was perceptive enough to recognize his good fortune. The Civil War was over and so was the anguish of Reconstruction. Slavery, western expansion, the slaughter of the Indians—all the major issues of the last half century had been resolved, at least in the minds of contemporary policy makers. America was on autopilot. As long as Garfield kept to his usual, moderate course, he could expect to reign untroubled for the next four, and quite possibly eight, years.

Garfield did relatively little in his 120 productive days as president, although he raised a few eyebrows when he appointed one of his Half-breed supporters to the post of Collector of Customs for the Port of New

York. The customs post, previously held by now Vice President Chester Arthur, had been a prime source of patronage jobs, kickbacks, and other "spoils" for the Stalwarts in the Republican Party. The appointment angered Arthur and several powerful Stalwart senators, but Garfield ignored their criticism. It was politics. They would get over it.

Unknown to Garfield, one man who wouldn't get over it was now in Washington, desperately trying to meet with the new president. His name was Charles Julius Guiteau, a con artist, blackmailer, and all-around unsuccessful deadbeat who was counting on a patronage job to revive his failing fortunes. He'd been an overbearing braggart since childhood; now he was also succumbing to delusions brought on by syphilis. Guiteau haunted the White House for months following the inauguration, an infuriatingly persistent, well-mannered madman, convinced that Garfield—whom he had never met—would name him either Foreign Minister to Austria or Counsel General for France. But ten grueling weeks of increasingly blunt rebuffs had worn Guiteau's self-confidence thin. He became convinced that his rejection was part of a Garfield plot to exclude all Stalwarts—Guiteau included—from patronage jobs. The popular press, which at that moment was lambasting Garfield for the Collector of Customs squabble, seemed to confirm Guiteau's suspicion.

What could Guiteau do? In mid-May, the solution came to him in a flash (which he later attributed to God): kill Garfield. This simple act would promote Chester Arthur to the presidency, and that would ensure that the Stalwarts would get their rightfully deserved patronage jobs. It would also, in Guiteau's humble estimation, "save the Republic."

Guiteau intended to become famous from Garfield's assassination, so he prepared for it with an eye toward history. First, he revised and expanded the manuscript of a book he had written several years earlier, *The Truth: A Companion to the Bible,* since he knew that demand for it would skyrocket once he had killed the president. He visited the District of Columbia jail where he knew he would be taken to assure himself that it was strong enough to repel any misguided lynch mob. (Guiteau believed the anger against him would pass and the American people would then hail him as their savior, paving the way for his own run for the presidency and then "ruler of the world.") Guessing that he might be muzzled by the authorities, he wrote letters to several prominent politicians and newspapers, carefully explaining his motives, which he planned to leave at the murder scene. Finally, he purchased the most powerful pistol he could find, a .44 caliber British Bulldog. He paid an extra dollar for one with an ivory handle because he wanted it to look good when it was displayed in a museum.

The preliminaries completed, Guiteau began stalking Garfield. He spent the entire month of June following him around the capital, waiting for just the right moment, his gun in one pocket and his packet of letters in the other. In hindsight, it's amazing that Guiteau needed a month. President Garfield was an easy target. He had no bodyguards and walked freely around Washington, often alone. Garfield felt that the leader of a Republic should mingle with the people he served, and most Americans agreed. The idea that a statesman might be assassinated in peacetime America was unimaginable.

On July 2, Guiteau learned that the president was leaving Washington by train for a summer vacation. Guiteau was nearly broke; he had to act now. Always mindful of the media, he put on a clean shirt. He arrived at the station ten minutes before Garfield, left his packet of letters near the newsstand, and had his boots shined. Then he took up a position outside the waiting room, just off the platform. Garfield obligingly entered only moments later. Guiteau approached from behind and fired two bullets from less than a yard away. He was a terrible shot. One bullet merely grazed Garfield's arm, the other hit him in the back about four inches from his spine.

With so much firepower hitting him from so little distance, Garfield should have hit the floor dead. Instead, he wasn't even unconscious. But Guiteau was unaware of that as he was hustled off to the jail that he had already visited and from which he expected to soon be released. "I am a Stalwart," he explained cheerfully to the policeman who accompanied him. "Arthur is now president of the United States."

That would have been good news to James Abram Garfield, who lay on the train-station floor in a pool of his own vomit, his new spring suit rapidly blackening with blood. It would have meant that he'd suffered a quick and merciful end. But Garfield, until recently the most fortunate man in America, who'd become president with such little effort, was about to have a run of very bad luck.

A gaggle of doctors quickly gathered around the stricken president and immediately made the first of what would be many incorrect diagnoses. They concluded that the bullet had ripped through one, if not several, of Garfield's internal organs. The president was finished, they all agreed. He would not live out the day. Hence, in the first twenty-four hours after the shooting, when aggressive medical treatment might have saved Garfield's life, he was instead left to lie in a hot White House bedroom, written off for dead.

But Garfield did not die. He lived through that first day, and the next, and the next... on and on and on. It would take the president eleven long, painful weeks to die, thanks to the combined efforts of some of America's highest-placed physicians.

The temperature and the humidity in the White House sickroom that July and August soared into the mid-nineties and stayed there, yet the doctors refused to move the president north to a cooler climate. It was only the first in a series of overcautious decisions that seemed designed to minimize the doctors' responsibility and maximize the president's misery.

Dr. D. Willard Bliss, one of Garfield's old neighbors from Ohio, took charge of the president's recovery. He was a competent surgeon and a member of the District Board of Health, but it appears that what qualified him most for the job was that he was the only one brazen enough to grab it.

Working on the assumption that important people need more doctors than the less fortunate, Dr. Bliss always had at least a half-dozen other physicians milling around the bed. This supporting cast changed continually over the long, hot summer. Mostly they did nothing but assure each other that the best action was no action at all.

The inept assassin's bullet had broken two ribs, shattered one of the president's vertebrae, and nicked an artery that fed the spleen, but it had not ruptured or even so much as bruised any internal organs. In fact, it was slowly being encysted in scar tissue and was of no harm to Garfield whatsoever. Yet from the start, even in the train-station waiting room, Garfield's wound was prodded and probed, first with dirty fingers, then with dirty instruments, in an attempt to find the bullet. Dr. Bliss got a heavy probe tipped with rough porcelain stuck in the fragments of one of Garfield's fractured ribs. He had to wrench it free, causing Garfield excruciating pain. Undaunted, Bliss and the others continued sticking things into the president. Most American physicians still scoffed at Louis Pasteur's twenty-year-old theory of bacterial infection. As a result, the daily insertion of unsterilized (and sometimes unwashed) fingers and instruments into Garfield's wound spread infection and ensured that it wouldn't heal.

Even electrical science was employed in the search for the harmless bullet. The doctors remembered Garfield's affinity for the telephone and asked Alexander Graham Bell to invent a metal detector that could scan the president's body. Bell dutifully came to Garfield's bedside, but his device proved worthless because the president lay on a bed with metal springs. When Bell told the doctors that Garfield would have to be moved, they refused. Bell was sent away.

Despite his strapping physique, Garfield had always been a picky eater. Now unable to keep down solid foods, the president was put on a diet of lime water, milk, and oatmeal, which he hated. The doctors supplemented this with a series of "nutrient enemas," a thick gruel of eggs, beef extract, and whiskey pumped up his rectum. It did no good at all. Dr. Bliss was especially proud of his enema treatments, telling the *Washington Star* in late August that it had "saved the president." By that time Garfield was already past the point of no return, his body so depleted of vitamins and minerals that it could never recover.

The doctors imposed a strict protocol on the White House sickroom. Garfield was scolded whenever he tried to talk, laugh, move, or exercise his brain. He had been an active, physical man who had amused his son by turning a cartwheel over his bed less than an hour before he was shot. The doctors demanded that he lie perfectly still. He had been a gregarious man, a born politician. The doctors sealed him off from the outside world. When he was allowed a rare visitor, talking was forbidden. One attempt by Garfield to talk to his wife "was met with a stern remonstrance from the male watchers," reported the *New York Tribune*. When Garfield asked the doctors if he could speak with someone—anyone—about government matters, they flatly refused. "We will not let him," Dr. Bliss informed the press. "We told him they were of very little importance."

To be fair, some of the blame for Garfield's misery rested squarely with Garfield. He lay there day after day, feverish, vomiting, barely able to sleep, in constant pain, with deadly infections slowly spreading through his body—and said nothing. Garfield had come up through adversity, was proud of his manly self-control, and believed in his doctors. They told him not to question decisions, he didn't. They told him not to speak, he obeyed. They told him not to move, he lay there, week after grueling week.

This, of course, made the doctors very happy. "I have never seen a more wonderfully patient sufferer," remarked one physician with approval. Garfield's self-control and unwavering obedience were favorite topics in the doctors' thrice-daily medical bulletins, which were devoured by the American people, hungry for any news. What had once been seen as Garfield's character flaws—his fatalism, his unwillingness to express emotion or be confrontational—were transformed by the doctors and a cooperative press into noble attributes that reflected well on the national character. The *New York Times* reported that "the wounded and possibly dying president has preserved the bearing of a soldier in the presence of peril and pain." The *New York Evening Mail* rhapsodized, "Lying patiently on a bed of suffering he has conquered the whole civilized world."

Garfield, who had barely been elected when healthy and who had done virtually nothing in office, was now the most popular man in America and the most popular president since Lincoln. His condition was *the* topic of conversation in the summer of 1881. It supported a boom industry in commemorative lithographs, the most fashionable being one of the president in bed, surrounded by his earnest and learned-looking doctors. Few American homes were without one.

Wounded and helpless, Garfield had become what he never could have been otherwise—a folk hero. "This worship will make him all-powerful," noted one of Garfield's colleagues, "if he lives."

By September 1, James Abram Garfield had had enough. His face was partially paralyzed, he had nearly drowned in his own mucus, his mind was wandering. Garfield's barrel-chested frame, normally a robust 210 pounds, had wasted away to 125 pounds in just nine weeks. The active, sociable president had slowly become a withered shell as he lay there silent, hot, lonely, and motionless, week after dreary, painful week.

Casting his heroic manliness aside, Garfield broke down and begged to be taken to the New Jersey shore, where he and his family had vacationed in healthier, happier times. The doctors were reluctant, but the president insisted. On September 6 his bed was mounted on special heavy-duty springs in a railroad car cooled with blocks of ice. Garfield was taken to Elberon, New Jersey, where his bed was carried to an upstairs room in a beachfront mansion. It was hoped that cool sea breezes would lift the president's spirits, but for the next two days the Jersey shore roasted under a record heat wave with temperatures up to a hundred degrees. It was even worse than Washington.

Garfield slid downhill fast. Besides the pain, vomiting, and delirium, he now exhibited a violent, hacking cough (the onset of pneumonia), a high fever, and painful spasms near the heart. The president was also clearly dying of blood poisoning, brought on by the continuous poking and by the decaying bone fragments in his body that the doctors had refused to remove. Still, the ever-optimistic Dr. Bliss predicted a miraculous recovery for his patient. In one of his last press conferences, he confidently reported that the president showed signs of improvement and that the Atlantic Ocean air would surely give him the vitality he needed to heal himself.

On the evening of September 19, Garfield awoke and began clawing at his chest. "Swaim!" he moaned to his attendant. "Can't you stop this? Oh, Swaim!" The nicked splenic artery had finally burst. The president sank into unconsciousness. Finally, eighty days after he'd been shot, he died.

Garfield's death caused an international outpouring of grief. A day of mourning was declared in the courts of Europe, the first ever for a citizen of a Republic. In America, which had been worked to a fever pitch by the press, the people exploded in the greatest outpouring of pity, grief, and anguish since the death of George Washington.

Garfield's casket was viewed by an estimated hundred thousand people in the Capitol rotunda. His body was then shipped to Cleveland, where it was entombed in a garish mausoleum that combined all the worst architectural excesses of the Gilded Age. Mosaics and bas-relief carvings illustrated every phase of the dead president's brief career. Inside, the stairway leading to his crypt was guarded by a heroic statue of Garfield carved from a single block of Italian marble.

Chester Arthur indeed became president of the United States, as Charles Guiteau had wished. But once in office, the former backslapping spoilsman rose above his unsavory past, surprising everyone. He declared a moratorium on patronage jobs, passed America's first civil-service reform act, vetoed the ban on Chinese immigration, and urged the prosecution of corrupt former associates accused of post office graft. Despite his efforts on behalf of the common good (or perhaps because of them), his own party denied him renomination to the presidency in 1884.

Meanwhile, Charles Guiteau had slowly come to understand that the American people did not regard him as their savior. In fact, they wanted to kill him, which would effectively end his plans to be the ruler of the world. Guiteau mounted a spirited defense at his trial, which he paid for by selling autographs for a dollar apiece. He explained to the jury that no human law could supersede a direct order from God. He argued that while he did shoot the president, he did not kill him; the doctors did. Finally, he maintained that "to hang a man in my mental condition would be a lasting disgrace to the American people." It was flawless logic but specious reasoning, and the jury didn't buy it. Charles Guiteau swung by his neck from a scaffold on June 30, 1882.

Garfield's doctors fared little better. Dr. Bliss, in particular, complained that his tireless efforts on behalf of the president had ruined his private practice. Congress was unsympathetic and slashed his fees, then slashed the fees of all the other doctors as well. The glory-loving Bliss, now the subject of abusive editorials, fell into a depression and died not long after his most famous patient.

The people's deification of Garfield collapsed almost as rapidly as his splenic artery. The mausoleum's honor guard was recalled by the same stingy Congress that had slashed the doctors' fees. The lithographs came off the walls and were dispatched to America's attics.

When President William McKinley was assassinated in 1901, the nation had a new chief executive on which to focus its sympathy and admiration. James Abram Garfield sank back into the obscurity from which he came, this time for good.

# 12

# Dead End

Edmonson County sits atop the central Kentucky karst, a limestone belt of rocky hillsides, smoky hollows, and deeply wooded glens. The Indians knew the region, as did the nameless people who came before them, for the karst limestone is honeycombed with magnificent caves. Travertine stalagmites, onyx draperies, and crystalline gypsum flowers have fascinated explorers and bewitched the curious for thousands of years. To these people the miles of passages must have seemed endless.

With the dawn of the twentieth century the caverns of central Kentucky began attracting a new breed of admirer—tourists. The advent of the automobile and paved roads made the caves not only accessible, but profitable. Mammoth Cave, the biggest of them all, was the magnet that drew the most people to Edmonson County. Its owners built a hotel above its entrance and an elevator to whisk its visitors effortlessly to the cavern below. The people who owned the land around Mammoth, poor farmers for the most part, looked on enviously.

Some entrepreneurs raided smaller caves for their onyx and gypsum to sell at souvenir stands along the road to Mammoth. Others, more ambitious, sought commercial-sized caves on their own properties and tried to siphon off visitors. But rival cave owners were always at a disadvantage, for Mammoth lay along Highway 70 between them and the nearest big town, Cave City. The secret to success, everyone knew, was location. The first person who could find a cave farther up the road than Mammoth would make a fortune.

Floyd Collins was looking for that cave. Sturdy, unflappable, with only a fifth-grade education, Collins had spent most of his thirty-seven years in Edmonson County and knew the miles of underground passages beneath it as well as anyone. He'd discovered a cavern on his own property, Crystal Cave, which was generally conceded to have the best formations of them all. But Crystal was far off Highway 70 and far beyond Mammoth. Tourists rarely visited.

Collins had a hunch, which he only confided to his kin, that all of the rival caves in the region—Great Onyx, Salts, Colossal, and even Mammoth itself—were interconnected. If he could find a cavern opening closer to Cave City than all of the others, he believed he could then find a passage that would link it to Crystal Cave.

Everyone in Edmonson County knew Collins and respected his skills. Privately, however, they worried about his recklessness. Collins would disappear into an unknown hole for hours, sometimes days, with nothing more than a battered kerosene lantern and a few cans of beans. Anyone who has ever explored a wild cave knows that *the* cardinal sin is to go in alone, but that's the way Floyd worked. He was self-reliant and independent, and he loved the solitude and quiet of the underground world, the beauty of its natural formations, and the adventure that exploring the unknown brought to his otherwise hardscrabble farm life.

In January 1925 Floyd found a promising sinkhole on the property of a neighbor, Beesley Doyle. It lay only a few hundred feet off Highway 70 and closer to Cave City than any other cavern; the perfect location for success. It was later dubbed "Sand Cave" by the press, but it was neither sandy nor a cave. It was a muddy, wet crack in the ground that corkscrewed down for hundreds of feet, no one knew where, and no one particularly wanted to find out. Even to experienced cave explorers—and there were many in Edmonson County—this miserable crevice looked menacing and dangerous, something best left alone. But Floyd Collins was bolder than most, and he was intrigued by the breeze blowing out of the cave's tiny entrance, a sure sign that large passages lay beyond the initial hellish squeeze. He blasted the hole with dynamite, waited a day for the dust to settle, then crawled in for a look.

Cave exploring is not for the fainthearted or claustrophobic, and Sand Cave tested the endurance of the most able. Collins found himself wiggling down into a tight, muddy passageway that twisted and turned through shattered rock and jumbled boulders. He squeezed through cracks and fissures barely wide enough to admit him. Solid limestone blocks pressed in as he squirmed through cold mud, using only his abdominal and thigh muscles, a human inchworm.

By about noon, Collins had satisfied himself that the cave did indeed lead to larger passages below, and he turned around and headed toward the surface. He was in the narrowest part of the cave—a horizontal fissure ten inches high and eighteen inches wide—when it happened. A small rock, the size of a football, hung from the unstable ceiling. It weighed only twenty-seven pounds. Collins accidentally pressed against it with his foot. In a moment, it fell out of position and wedged tightly against his left ankle, immobilizing him. No matter how hard he wriggled or twisted, he could not break free.

Collins was on his back, pinned in the tight squeeze, his arms trapped against his sides by the surrounding limestone, his upturned face sticking out into the bottom of the narrow, muddy chute that eventually spiraled to the surface. Any movement on his part triggered showers of dirt and debris that poured onto his face. Icy water, trickling down from above, soaked him continuously. The breeze that had intrigued Floyd now blew steadily over his body, chilling him to the bone. It was Friday, January 30, 1925. Floyd Collins was buried alive.

By the next morning Beesley Doyle had become sufficiently alarmed at Floyd's absence to take a walk out to Sand Cave. He found Collins but couldn't find a way to help him, a problem that vexed all the rescuers who would eventually slither into Sand Cave to try their luck. Most of these men, like Doyle, were out of shape, occasionally drunk, and terrified of the place. They would only get a certain distance into the muddy crevice before exhaustion, discomfort, and fear drove them back. Few actually made it down to Floyd—who was only about sixty feet below the surface—and those who did were stymied by his cramped surroundings. There was barely enough space at the bottom of the chute to scrape muck into a coffee can. There was no room to swing a hammer or dig with a shovel. Worst of all, the rock that had pinned Floyd was lodged at the back end of the squeeze that his body now jammed shut.

The only good thing was that Floyd's head was out in the open, which meant he could be fed. Collins was tough and strong, and as long as he could eat and drink, chances were good that he would stay alive until his rescuers could figure a way to get him out.

News of Floyd's predicament spread quickly along the ridges and hollows. Men converged on the sinkhole from as far away as Louisville, most with a sincere desire to help. Unfortunately, anger quickly flared between Floyd's neighbors and those from outside Edmonson County, derisively called "outlanders." The neighbors argued that the outlanders knew nothing about caves and should stay clear while Floyd's friends dug him out. The men from Louisville argued that aggressive technology and engineering—not primitive digging—was the only way to free Floyd. Both groups had their champions and neither had any respect for the other. While they wasted days bickering and sometimes threatening to hit each other, Floyd lay below in the darkness. Loneliness, terror, hypothermia, malnutrition, and constant pain gradually ate away his strength.

In 1925 Kentucky cave country was still a physically remote region, and it took several days for the commonwealth authorities to realize that a knot of chaos was rapidly unraveling in Edmonson County. Meanwhile—private enterprise being quicker than government bureaucracy—every do-gooder with an idea and a means of transportation was flocking to Sand Cave to try to save Floyd. Two gravestone cutters offered to go down and chisel Collins loose. A Louisville builder wanted to melt away the limestone above Floyd with an oxyacetylene torch. Another wanted to blast Floyd free with an air hammer. The directionless mob outside Sand Cave, when they weren't cursing each other, rejected these ideas. Only three options were deemed worth considering: Dig a vertical shaft to a point lower than Floyd, then break through into Sand Cave and rescue him from below; thread a harness underneath Floyd's arms, attach it to a rope running up the cave, and yank him free; or have one man stand in the chute and dig Floyd out slowly, one coffee canful of muck at a time.

While the merits of these options were endlessly argued, the well-being of Floyd escaped the squabbling, leaderless crowd. It never occurred to them to run a telephone receiver down to Collins to communicate with him or to rig a garden hose so that the starving man could regularly receive warm water or broth, although both could easily have been done. Even the idea of picking a team of slim, sober men who could go in to provision Floyd was beyond the imagination of his self-styled saviors. William "Skeets" Miller, a Louisville reporter who volunteered to run a string of electric lights down to Floyd (and thereby secure an eye-popping first-person account for his newspaper), only had the idea at the last moment to place the final bulb on Floyd's neck, thereby providing the shivering man some measure of heat. On the way back to the surface, Skeets ruefully noted that nearly every crack in the cave was stuffed with food, blankets, and whiskey bottles by those who claimed to have brought these to Floyd, but who never got that far.

The mob finally rejected the rescue shaft method because it would take too long to dig and would possibly weaken the already unstable cave. The harness-and-rope method was tried—once—and then abandoned. Floyd, who accepted that his foot would probably be torn off, screamed that the tension was instead ripping his body in two. He was probably correct. That left only the laborious coffee-can-digging option, and it must be said that Floyd's rescuers went at it with gusto. Skeets Miller, who genuinely admired Floyd's durability, was frequently in the chute and at one point had enough muck scraped away to worm a jack and crowbar next to Floyd's body in an attempt to lever the rock off of his foot. Miller got it to move, but not far enough; the wood blocks that supported the jack kept slipping out at the critical moment. For the rest of his life, Skeets would never forgive himself for not thinking to wire or tape the blocks together into a stable base. It was one of many little oversights that kept Collins pinned in freezing muck as time inexorably ticked away.

By now it was Tuesday, February 3. Floyd had been trapped in his miserable, muddy tomb for five days. His stamina was waning, sapping what little ability he had to use his own strength to help push free, occasionally leaving him delirious. In short, Floyd Collins was dying. On the plus side, the Kentucky National Guard had finally arrived, bringing order to the chaos above, chasing away the pickpockets and moonshiners. Now there would surely be enough trained, brave men to go down into the pit and dig Floyd out.

143

Unfortunately, the constant traffic in the cave had gradually made its walls and ceiling dangerously unstable. On early Wednesday morning, just as a rescue team was preparing to enter the cave, a ceiling section about twelve feet in front of Floyd collapsed. Floyd's neighbors, by now exhausted and terrified of a cave-in, scurried for safety, ignoring Floyd's pleading cries of "Don't leave me!" from behind the rubble. The outlanders, who had never favored the coffee-can-digging approach, seized the opportunity to declare Sand Cave off limits and announce that a second shaft was the only way to rescue Floyd.

Had anyone looked closely, they would have discovered a crawl space through the loose cave rubble, half-hidden in the shadows, that would have at least allowed them to continue to feed Floyd. But the frightened, tired men never noticed it. To them it seemed as if all of terrible Sand Cave was about to collapse on their heads. They had given up. Now it was up to the outlanders to save Floyd Collins with their engineering and technology.

While Floyd's rescuers whipsawed between near success and failure, Skeets Miller's stories had been picked up by the Associated Press and reprinted in over twelve hundred newspapers nationwide, often on front pages beneath screaming headlines. Reporters from Bowling Green and Lexington were soon circulating among the crowd at Sand Cave, followed by journalists from Nashville, Cincinnati, St. Louis, Atlanta, Chicago, Washington, and New York. The American public, it quickly became clear, couldn't get enough of the story. Women sent letters proposing marriage to Floyd; one even offered to crawl into the cave for the ceremony. City folks crowded around store windows that displayed the latest rescue bulletins. President Calvin Coolidge followed Floyd's terrible plight from the White House. Talent agents vied to be the first to book Floyd for a lecture tour once he had been set free and recovered from the ordeal.

The ongoing saga at Sand Cave was an economic bonanza for the mass media, which obligingly did everything it could to keep the story hot. A pool of fifty reporters from sixteen big-city papers and several foreign countries was soon churning out copy from the rescue site. A primitive radio station was trucked to Sand Cave to broadcast regular bulletins; newsreel crews were flown in by six Hollywood studios. In the rush for bankable copy, journalistic ethics became as muddy as the would-be rescuers stumbling out of Floyd's sinkhole. When the reporters couldn't get enough news, they made it up.

In contrast to Floyd's continued isolation, the hillsides surrounding Sand Cave were clogged with people. Even by the end of the second day of his entrapment the throng had reached over a hundred, many of them curiosity seekers who were more interested in the diversion than in the well-being of Floyd Collins. By Wednesday, the day of the collapse, the crowd had grown to well over two hundred. By the weekend, with the media juggernaut at full throttle, a flood of humanity had descended on Sand Cave, intrigued by what they had read, hoping for a peek at the helpless victim.

On Sunday, February 8, over four thousand cars from twenty different states trekked to Sand Cave, in addition to countless buggies, wagons, horses, and mules. Highway 70 boasted a four-mile, bumper-to-bumper traffic jam. An estimated twenty-five thousand visitors that day bought hot dogs, hamburgers, popcorn, balloons, soft drinks, and folding chairs from vendors who had set up carts and stands around the cave's entrance. Con men and jugglers worked the crowd for donations. The popular favorite of the afternoon was Floyd's father, who told anyone within earshot that his son's torment was a test of faith sent from God and who also sold pictures of Floyd for a dollar apiece. A stranger chancing upon the carnival would find it difficult to believe that sixty feet beneath it a human being was dying.

In the beginning, the idea that Floyd Collins might starve to death before his rescuers reached him seemed absurd. The National Guard had confidently predicted that the rescue shaft would reach Floyd in thirty-six hours, by Thursday the 5th or Friday the 6th, at the latest. It was only when the digging began that they realized that their technology was useless and that their engineering wasn't much help either. Modern tools such as steam shovels, pneumatic drills, and even dynamite had to be abandoned because they might cause the nearby cave to collapse onto Floyd. The entire six-foot-square, sixty-foot-deep shaft would have to be dug using only picks and spades.

Thursday passed, then Friday, Saturday, Sunday. The weather turned unusually warm, followed by steady, heavy rains. Water poured into the deepening shaft, forcing the men to dig in mud a foot deep, the walls repeatedly caving in. No one spoke of how the increased precipitation might affect Floyd, but anyone who had been in Sand Cave knew that once water trickled down to the level of Floyd's face it would have nowhere else to go.

Monday passed, then Tuesday, Wednesday, Thursday. Floyd Collins had been trapped for thirteen days. He hadn't eaten in over a week. Could he possibly still be alive? The rescuers hooked a radio receiver to the electric cord that Skeets Miller had dragged into the cave a week earlier and listened. Regular clicks and crackles came from the light bulb that still glowed against Floyd's neck, indicating that Floyd was either asleep or unconscious and breathing twelve times a minute. A weaker man would have died of shock, thirst, starvation, exposure, exhaustion, or pain. A more fortunate man would have been quickly crushed under a cave-in or suffocated in mud. Floyd Collins was neither. Amazingly, he had survived.

Unfortunately, the pit was still not quite deep enough and no one was offering to go into Sand Cave to try to find a way under the collapsed ceiling. Floyd would have to keep surviving on his own a little longer. Despite the frantic efforts of the pit diggers, muck and gravel slowed their progress to four inches an hour. Limestone boulders had to be laboriously pounded to pieces and dug out by hand. Loose material was falling in from the sides so constantly that many feared that the entire pit might collapse.

The diggers stayed at it for another four days, then drove a shaft laterally from the fifty-five foot level. On Monday afternoon, February 16, after 312 hours of back-breaking labor, Floyd's rescuers finally broke through into Sand Cave. They immediately realized, to their embarrassment, that they were still six feet above Floyd, in the same chute that Miller and the other early rescuers had primitively scraped with their coffee cans. The whole advantage of the pit had been lost. Floyd was there to greet his rescuers, his mouth open in a grin, dead. The coroner later ruled that Floyd had probably passed away three days earlier, on Friday the 13th.

The noble—if tragically bungled—spirit of self-sacrifice that fueled the efforts to rescue Floyd Collins evaporated once it was learned that he was no longer alive. Homer, Floyd's younger brother, asked that the body be removed from Sand Cave so that Floyd could receive a proper burial, but no one wanted to spend any more time in the treacherous pit. Sand Cave's entrance was sealed shut, the pit was filled in, and Floyd was left where he was. Beesley Doyle, recognizing a business opportunity, put up a big sign—200 YARDS AWAY THE BODY OF FLOYD COLLINS IS IMPRISONED IN SAND CAVE—set up a ticket booth, and charged fifty cents to anyone who wanted to take a peek. Floyd's dad began advertising Crystal Cave as "Floyd Collins Crystal Cave" in the hope of attracting more visitors. A maudlin ballad, *The Death of Floyd Collins,* sold over three million copies.

Homer Collins hit the vaudeville circuit with a slide lecture about the failed rescue. After eight months he'd raised enough money to pay a mining crew to reopen the pit and drag out Floyd, whose ears and face had been partly eaten by cave crickets. Floyd's body was embalmed and buried next to the Collins homestead with a huge sta-lagmite to mark the grave. Beesley Doyle, claiming his rights as property owner, kept the Rock of Death and Floyd's left shoe and displayed them in his ticket booth, where they were popular attractions.

Despite his burial, Floyd's postmortem humiliation was far from over. Two years after Floyd's death, his dad sold Crystal Cave to a local dentist, with the secret under-standing that the dentist could have Floyd's body as well. To the horror of Floyd's surviving siblings, the dentist dug up Floyd, re-embalmed him, dressed him in a suit and white gloves, and displayed the corpse in a glass-lidded coffin in the main concourse of Crystal Cave. This boosted attendance considerably. Somewhere along the way Floyd was christened "The World's Greatest Cave Explorer," although how someone so great could have gotten himself into such a bad situation was a subject tactfully avoided by the guides.

In March 1929 Floyd was stolen. Police found him a day later, wrapped in a gunnysack and thrown into some bushes near the cave's entrance. His left leg, the one that had been trapped, was missing. It was never found.

Floyd was returned to his attendance-boosting duties, although now his casket had a metal lid that was locked at night. Visitors, however, could still get a peek if they tipped the guide. Floyd remained a public curiosity until 1961, when the National Parks Service bought Crystal Cave and closed it to all but professional cavers. Humidity and time continued to eat away at the coffin, and in 1989 the Collins family finally decided to remove Floyd and bury him in the ground, literally, for the third time. He now lies in little Flint Ridge Cemetery, a hundred yards off Crystal Cave Road, next to his father.

In the early 1970s a caving team finally found a connection between Mammoth and Crystal Caves, verifying what Floyd Collins had suspected (or perhaps knew) fifty years earlier. However, try as they might, cavers have never found a link between Sand Cave and Crystal Cave—or any other.

# 13

# Hang the Jew

APRIL 27 WAS CONFEDERATE MEMORIAL DAY, A LEGAL HOLI-
day across the South in 1913. Atlanta, Georgia, marked
the occasion with a parade. Pretty Mary Phagan, a week
shy of her fourteenth birthday, came to the city to watch
the festivities.

Mary lived in Marietta, eighteen miles north. The trip
was routine for her. Although barely in her teens, Mary
had been forced by poverty to take a job in Atlanta, at a
brass-stamping machine in the National Pencil Company
factory. On her way to the parade she stopped at the factory to collect her pay. Before she left she was clubbed
over the head, dragged into the basement, and garroted to
death.

One of the last people to see Mary Phagan alive was
Leo M. Frank, age twenty-nine, the factory's managing
superintendent. A Texan by birth, he was a colorless,
rigid man, a Cornell graduate, and a Jew. Slightly built,

with bulging eyes and a nervous disposition, he was vaguely described as "unpleasant" by the press of his day. He was a mysterious and unfamiliar creature to the Deep South.

Leo Frank was in his office, working on the factory's weekly financial report, when Mary stopped in to collect her wages. Five days later, when he was arrested, both the police and the press had a vested interest in proving he had killed her.

The police needed someone to blame. Thirteen women had been murdered in Atlanta over the past three years; all the cases were unsolved. The victims had been black—and thus of minor importance to the 1913 Atlanta police—but the white public was concerned that anyone capable of killing black women could some day start killing white women. The police had done nothing, and now a virginal white Anglo-Saxon Protestant girl was dead.

The press needed someone to blame. In 1913 Atlanta had three daily newspapers, all locked in a brutal circulation war. All three recklessly exploited the Leo Frank case in a shameless campaign to attract readers. Rumors became fact, innuendo became "scoops." Screaming headlines demanded Leo Frank's conviction. One paper ran a cruelly retouched photo of Frank captioned MONSTER.

The white people of Georgia, too, needed someone to blame. When the police discovered Mary Phagan's body they had automatically arrested the night watchman at the pencil factory—a black man—but the public was unsatisfied with the choice. There was something inexplicable and alien about this crime, something that struck very deep at southern notions of honor and womanhood.

The general feeling was that Mary's death merited a more heinous perpetrator.

That left Leo Frank, a strange-looking, unemotional Yankee Jew, the nephew of a millionaire, and the superintendent of a factory that paid Gentile girls like Mary Phagan twelve cents an hour. To many white people in Atlanta, he was the embodiment of evil.

Actually, the death of Mary Phagan was neither inexplicable nor alien. Evidence strongly suggested that she had been murdered for her weekly wages, a mere $1.20, by a man named Jim Conley, who worked as a sweeper at the pencil factory. He was a black man with a long arrest record, but in the peculiar dynamics that shaped the Leo Frank case he became an ally of the poor white South against the rich Yankee Jew.

Conley was the principal witness for the state against Leo Frank. On the witness stand he told the Christian people of Atlanta what they wanted to hear. He brushed aside the defense's dramatic revelation that Mary Phagan, contrary to popular belief, had not been raped. "Pervert" Leo Frank, Conley countered, had nevertheless intended to rape the girl but had obviously been interrupted before he could complete the terrible act. The prosecution offered no proof of Conley's assertion, which contradicted the crime scene evidence and everything known about Leo Frank's character. But to the public, who had already deified Mary Phagan as a dishonored damsel and damned Leo Frank as a "lecherous Jew," it made sense.

Leo Frank's trial took the entire month of August, and not once in the twenty-six days of testimony did the temperature in Atlanta fall below ninety degrees. Judge

Roan's sweltering courtroom had its windows thrown
open to the street, and through them poured the mob
that wanted Leo Frank dead. They surrounded the courthouse and pressed against the windowsills, cheering and
applauding the prosecution, heckling and booing the
defense, shouting death threats at Leo Frank and the jury.
"Hang the Jew or we'll hang you!" they chanted. The
police made no attempt to disperse them.

Under these circumstances, a jury of twelve men
found Leo Frank guilty after less than four hours of deliberation. The next day Judge Roan sentenced Leo Frank to
hang, and the white population of Atlanta erupted in
spontaneous celebration. Atlantans danced for an hour in
front of the National Pencil Company factory. The great
news was chalked up on the scoreboard at the baseball
stadium. A public barbecue was held in honor of the
prosecuting attorney and the jury. Judge Roan confided to
an associate, "Why, if Christ and all his angels came to
show this man innocent, they would still vote him guilty."
Then he denied Leo Frank a retrial.

For the next two years Leo Frank awaited execution in the
Atlanta jail and was the subject of endless public curiosity. At least a hundred Georgians a day came and asked
the gate guards if they could see "the strangler, Frank."
(They were politely turned away.) More milled about the
prison's outside walls, seeking some vantage point from
which they could catch a glimpse of the timid, artless
arch-murderer.

The public's continued fascination with Frank flabbergasted his bewildered attorneys, still incredulous that
their client had been convicted. They'd believed that once

Frank was behind bars the mob fever would die down; then they could seek to overturn his conviction in the higher courts. But the press, the police, and the public were not going to let that happen. Mary Phagan had become a symbol to the white people of Georgia, particularly to the poverty-stricken tenant farmers and mill hands who saw in her a reflection of their own desperate lives. The factories and crop lien system that kept them penniless were the work of New York Jew Yankees—everyone knew that—and now that they had a Jew, sentenced to death in a court of American law, they were determined to see that his execution was carried out.

Their hate was fueled by a man who, perhaps not surprisingly, was the shadowy exploiter of Georgia's poor that Leo Frank was supposed to be. Thomas E. Watson, a white Anglo-Saxon Protestant, a son of Georgia soil, and the undisputed political boss of the state, had been elected twenty-five years earlier to the United States Congress. At that time he was a champion of Georgia's oppressed, black and white, Christian and Jew. But his political star fell as quickly as it had risen, and in a calculated move to maintain his grip on power he abandoned his platform of class solidarity for one that championed white supremacy. By glorifying the southern status quo—isolationist, provincial, and white-run—it extinguished any hope for the poor of Georgia to improve their lives. But given nothing else, they embraced it.

Alcoholic and half-mad, "Old Tom" was a brilliant propagandist who well understood the dark corners of the white Georgian mind. He owned two widely read publications, the *Jeffersonian* weekly newspaper and monthly magazine, and in their pages he preached his message of nativism and hate. Like most outside Atlanta, he had ignored the Leo Frank case during the trial because he believed that Frank would be acquitted. But the conviction, its widespread popular support, and the continuing attempts by Frank's attorneys to overturn it gave Watson an issue that he could twist to his political advantage.

Watson tore into those who would defend this "rich depraved Sodomite" and "filthy perverted Jew of New York" with seething venom. "Frank belongs to the Jewish aristocracy," he wrote, "and it was determined by rich Jews that no aristocrat of their race should die for the death of a working girl!" Watson called attention to Frank's "bulging, satyr eyes" and "animal jaw" and declared that Frank had "a ravenous appetite for the forbidden fruit—a lustful eagerness enhanced by the racial novelty of a girl of the uncircumcised." He luridly suggested that Mary Phagan had died defending her virtue from a Jewish conspiracy to "mongrelize" southern white womanhood.

Whatever hope Leo Frank had for justice vanished once Tom Watson began his crusade. The state courts and politicians were cowed by the mobs who read the *Jeffersonian* and yowled for Frank's neck. Every tribunal that reviewed the Frank case expressed doubts about its validity but refused to overturn the verdict. Watson's lurid prose kept the pressure on. "How much longer is the blood of little Mary Phagan to cry in vain to Heaven for vengeance?" he demanded. "Rise, people of Georgia!"

On June 10, 1915, the Georgia prison board denied Leo Frank his final plea for clemency and set June 22 as his execution date. Frank had one last hope. Georgia governor John Slaton, whose final day in office would be the day before the execution, had executive power to grant clemency. Slaton had dreams of going on to the United States Senate; he also had a conscience. On June 21 he stunned Georgia by not only commuting Frank's sentence to life imprisonment, but by releasing his own lengthy review of the same presenting evidence that had been withheld from the jury, evidence that indicated that Leo Frank was an innocent man.

Leo Frank was not in Atlanta to hear the good news. Governor Slaton had smuggled him 150 miles south to a prison farm in Milledgeville the day before he ordered the commutation. It turned out to be a prudent move.

Not surprisingly, the white people of Atlanta were not interested in hearing that Leo Frank might be innocent. They were interested in killing him, and now their own governor had cheated them of their prey. The mood in Atlanta was ugly as night fell. An angry mob of over five thousand gathered on the statehouse lawn. Informed that Frank had been moved out of the city and beyond their reach, they cried, "Slaton, Slaton, King of the Jews!" and moved en mass toward Atlanta's South Side—its Jewish residential district.

Alerted to the approaching danger, Atlanta's thirty-five hundred Jewish residents shuttered their businesses and locked themselves in their homes, cowering in terror. Many fled the city. Their foresight ensured that there would be no Jewish sacrifices in Atlanta that night. The frenzied crowd, denied casual victims, turned its awful energy to the next logical target—the governor's mansion. John Slaton, Georgia's most popular governor since the Civil War, found himself besieged in his house by a torch-carrying mob armed with knives, guns, blackjacks, hatchets, and a basket of dynamite. Cries of "Jew lover!" and "Lynch him!" rent the night, and only the timely arrival of the Georgia militia with fixed bayonets saved Slaton from death.

While Slaton was being hanged and shot in effigy all over Georgia, others were planning more direct action. A group of over a hundred men met at Mary Phagan's grave, named themselves the Knights of Mary Phagan, and pledged to avenge her murder. They were all responsible fathers, wage-earners, and church-goers. They were going to kill Leo Frank.

With Tom Watson's incendiary spew to guide them ("Lynch law is God's law!") the Knights organized a necktie party unmatched in American history in audacity and efficiency. On the night of August 16 they drove boldly into Milledgeville, cut the telephone lines, broke through the prison gates, overpowered the guards, and seized Leo Frank. The entire operation took less than ten minutes. The lynch mob then drove 175 miles to Marietta, to a spot overlooking the house where Mary Phagan had been born, and at dawn they hanged Leo Frank from an oak tree.

When the police arrived an hour later, over a thousand people were already crowding the site, gawking at the dead man. The rope binding Frank's feet was cut into pieces for souvenirs, as were the sleeves of his nightshirt. Snapshots were taken of Leo Frank's dangling body, which were turned into postcards and sold in Georgia drugstores for the next twenty years. Once Frank had been cut down, one of the bystanders drove his heel into the dead man's face, stamping it again and again.

A festive spirit prevailed in Georgia that day. In Marietta, "Fiddling John" Corcoran played "The Ballad of Mary Phagan" to crowds who had come from all over the state to visit the murder site:

> She fell down on her knees
> To Leo Frank and pled
> He picked up a plank from the trash pile
> And beat her over the head. . . .

> Judge Roan passed the sentence
> He passed it very well
> The Christian doers of heaven
> Sent Leo Frank to hell.

Under the headline THE VOICE OF THE PEOPLE IS THE VOICE OF GOD Tom Watson trotted out all his old shibboleths in a final vitriolic diatribe. "Womanhood is made safer everywhere," he crowed. "Let Jew libertines take notice . . . the wages of sin is death." The issue covering Leo Frank's murder was the best selling in *Jeffersonian* history.

Georgia's new governor, Nat Harris, announced his intention to apprehend the lynchers. His office was immediately flooded with letters threatening the governor's life. No efforts were ever made.

Leo Frank's body was put on display in a Jewish-owned Atlanta funeral home, under threats that it would otherwise be burned. In the ten hours that it was on view, an estimated fifteen thousand people came to stare at the mutilated corpse.

Shortly after Leo Frank's death, the mayor of Atlanta, James Woodward, defended the lynching at a governors' conference in California. "The people felt it was up to them to take the law into their hands," he explained. "When it comes to a woman's honor, there is no limit we will not go to avenge and protect."

Mary Phagan had never been protected while she was alive. But she was honored in death, on the anniversary of her murder, every year for a decade, when a procession of the poor made a pilgrimage to her grave. Marietta Camp #763 of the United Confederate Veterans erected a monument at the site.

Nearby, the Knights of Mary Phagan stood a twenty-four-hour guard beside the oak tree from which they had hanged Leo Frank, convinced that government officials corrupted by "Jew money" would try to cut it down. They needn't have bothered. The tree stood for nearly fifty years.

The county courthouse politics of Tom Watson and his cronies, now firmly in control of the state legislature, did little to stop the exploitation of child labor in Georgia. Many businesses left the state after the lynching of Leo Frank. Without factories to employ them, the poor grew poorer. Factory girls who kept their jobs worked for pitiful wages. The serfdom of unskilled labor in Georgia would be a scandal for decades to come.

Former governor John Slaton never reached the United States Senate. He was forced to leave Georgia for his own safety immediately after he'd commuted Leo Frank's death sentence. He didn't dare return for over four years. His political career was finished.

Tom Watson's career, in contrast, was back on track. The people of Georgia elected him to the United States Senate in 1920, sweeping Watson into office with 58 percent of the vote. Two idle years later, drunk and obese, he died. When his funeral was held in Atlanta, Tom Watson's coffin was overshadowed by an eight-foot-tall cross of roses sent by the Ku Klux Klan.

# 14

# Prophet of Rubber

CHARLES GOODYEAR INVENTED VULCANIZED RUBBER. THAT may not sound very exciting until you reflect that automobiles, bicycles, and almost every modern sport and outdoor activity would not exist without his work. He was a bare bones, hands-on inventor, full of pluck and perseverance. His family endured privations and humiliations almost beyond belief. His life was worn threadbare by public-spirited efforts to advance the best interests of humankind. And in return Charles Goodyear was exploited by the businessmen he made wealthy, shunned by the people he served, and mocked by nearly everyone.

Charles Goodyear did not invent rubber per se, which is only coagulated sap drawn from tropical trees. The substance had been a curiosity for centuries, but it didn't enter the commercial world until the 1820s when Charles Macintosh, a Glasgow chemist, made waterproof boots and raincoats by sandwiching a thin layer of the sticky gum between two pieces of canvas cloth.

Rubber, however, was unsuited for the climate extremes of the United States. In the winter it would freeze rock-hard and then snap like a dry twig. In the summer it would melt into a foul-smelling goo that stuck to everything, including anyone foolish enough to touch it. Items made from rubber would sag out of shape and then have to be buried to get rid of the horrible stink.

Still, rubber possessed an irresistible attraction. Here was a substance that could shed water and oil, that could absorb shocks and spring back to its original shape. To an America entering the Industrial Age, it was tantalizing. Many tried their hand at making and selling rubber goods—all failed. Factories and stores were opened, then abandoned; men were hired, then thrown out of work; millions of dollars were invested, then lost. By the early 1830s the honeymoon was over. Saggy, sticky, foul-smelling rubber products were hated by the public and so were the people who sold them. Every sensible inventor and manufacturer either abandoned rubber altogether or was looking for a way to cut losses and get out, quick.

That left the field wide open for someone like Charles Goodyear. He was a small, sickly man with a sallow complexion, faltering limbs, and a feeble constitution. Yet inside his rickety frame breathed an iron-willed optimist who believed God had put him on earth to help mankind. How that would happen he didn't know, but he was certain it was preordained. Few others shared his certainty. Goodyear was perpetually broke, with nothing to show for his life but poor business sense, chronic ill health, and persistent bad luck. He was frequently in jail, which was where debtors were sent in the 1800s until they could pay their bills.

In 1834, in a rare moment of solvency, Goodyear visited a Manhattan store displaying rubber life preservers. The prevention of drowning was one of Goodyear's minor obsessions, but the owner confided that the business was about to go bankrupt; rubber was useless. Goodyear was shocked that the rubber industry hadn't solved its production problems before it began selling products. (Goodyear would be doing it himself soon enough.) He was also entranced with rubber's elasticity, which he saw as a gift to humankind from God. Suddenly he realized that rubber, humankind, and God needed help. He vowed that he, Charles Goodyear, would be the man who would make rubber useful. It was a vision that he would hold unwavering, through years of disaster and personal tragedy, for the rest of his life.

The secret, as Goodyear saw it, was to combine raw rubber with some other ingredient that would "absorb" its objectionable qualities. Of course, the greatest industrial chemists of his day had also thought of this simple approach, tried it, and failed. That did not discourage the ever-confident Charles Goodyear. He believed that what intelligent research could not discover, accident could. With no knowledge of chemistry and no scientific training, completely ignorant of the obstacles that lay before him and bereft of any particular approach, he was perfect for the job.

For two years Goodyear single-mindedly kneaded rubber with whatever ingredients he could find, hoping to stumble across the magic mixture. His tools were his fingers and his wife's rolling pin. No one outside his immediate family offered him any hope of success. That they supported him at all is a testament to family devotion rarely equaled in modern times, since Charles Goodyear gave his wife and children only heartbreak in return. Any money that he made was poured into the bottomless pit of his rubber experiments. Six of his twelve children would eventually die from diseases brought on by their poverty. Those who survived had to dig half-grown potatoes for food and gather sticks for fuel. Goodyear pawned nearly all of his family's possessions, including his wife's dinner plates and his children's schoolbooks, to pay off his creditors. (He later made his wife a new set of plates out of rubber.) When he was sick, as he often was, he continued his experiments from his bed. When he was healthy he was either being hassled for money or thrown into jail.

Like any visionary, Goodyear was a tireless publicist for his cause. He carried rubber samples with him everywhere, even in prison, showing them to anyone who displayed the slightest interest. "There is probably no other inert substance," he wrote earnestly, "which so excites the mind." He made handbills out of rubber, trumpeting its marvelous virtues and "surpassing beauty," and posted them on walls and in storefront windows wherever he went. To test the durability of his product, Goodyear made a three-piece suit out of rubber and wore it until his body heat destroyed it. We can only guess what his neighbors thought of the smell.

Goodyear's indefatigable enthusiasm was partly to blame for his unending strife. Every time he stumbled upon a mixture or process that offered even the most meager promise, he would coax some equally meager capital out of a friend or investor with assurances of imminent success. He would then begin to manufacture rubber goods, announce this news to the public, and invariably end up penniless and in jail when the rubber inevitably froze or melted. After several false triumphs, Charles Goodyear and his damnable rubber were avoided like the plague by anyone with investment capital. It was considered bad for one's business reputation to be associated with Charles Goodyear.

For four years Goodyear tirelessly searched for the philosopher's stone that would transform rubber into something tough and durable, yet he was no closer to its discovery than when he'd begun. Goodyear moved his impoverished family into a shack on the grounds of an abandoned rubber factory. He invited his brother and his wife to join them because he needed their furniture. Goodyear spent all his time in the empty plant, laboriously making rubber goods that melted, or froze, or stunk.

His friends and relatives encouraged him to give up, arguing that if Charles Goodyear couldn't make rubber useful after so much time and effort, the problem must be insoluble. They urged him to apply his admirable energies to some gainful occupation, something that would feed his wife and children. Goodyear merely turned his attention back to his experiments, confident as always that the next batch would provide the answer he had been searching for.

Then Goodyear got a break, one of the few he would get in his life. For several months he had been toying with sulfur as an additive, noting that it dried the sticky surface of rubber and made it possible to produce thin items like tablecloths and sheets. As usual he overestimated its worth, ballyhooed it to the press, and then was left bankrupt when the thicker goods fell apart. In January 1839 he was pondering one of these failed pieces in a friend's kitchen when he accidentally dropped it onto a hot stove. The rubber, to his shock, didn't melt. It charred and it smelled awful, but it was dry, tough, and pliant. He took the piece home and nailed it to the wall outside his back door. Despite the sub-freezing temperature, the next morning the rubber was still flexible.

Here at last was the accidental breakthrough Goodyear had been chasing for five years. He called the new material "metallic gum-elastic" and showed the piece to everyone he could. No one paid any attention. No one wanted anything to do with yet another Charles Goodyear crackpot claim about rubber.

Goodyear had discovered a process that was worth millions, but he couldn't explain why it worked. Investors would be enticed if he could produce consistent results, but he couldn't do that either. How much heat? For how long? He needed answers, but he was sick and broke and had no access to a laboratory to continue his experiments, and he couldn't afford to pay for lab space even if it were available. But Goodyear realized that if he gave up on the secret he had stumbled across, it would be lost. He decided to carry on alone.

For five more years Goodyear battled poverty, ridicule, and the rapidly declining health of himself and his family to convince someone that he had created a marketable product. He used heat sources wherever he could find them, conducting pathetic experiments using his wife's saucepans and teakettle. The neighbors became familiar with the sound of Goodyear nailing rubber samples to the outside of his house at night. He would wander around Boston, his pockets full of rubber, begging shops and factories to let him use their ovens or furnaces after hours. When they kicked him out, he built bonfires from brushwood and stumps gathered from surrounding fields. When he was thrown in jail for debt, he would bring along samples that he would heat over a candle.

Goodyear's fourth child died, and the inventor was too poor to bury him in even a cheap pine box. His family now lived off of food provided by neighbors. Still, Goodyear's vision never wavered, his faith never faltered. "Duty bound to beg in earnest," he wrote, "sooner than the discovery should be lost to the world." The certainty of success, Goodyear believed, warranted extreme sacrifices.

He experimented endlessly, afraid to sleep, afraid he would die before his process was perfected. And miraculously, slowly, the years of tireless effort began producing promising results. By the fall of 1842 his blistered, burnt, and melted samples were being replaced by specimens that were as good or better than his original. Goodyear's brother could see what was happening and ordered Charles to keep his mouth shut. This time there would be no rush to production and no public humiliation. Late in 1843 Goodyear applied for a patent, and on June 15, 1844—ten years after he'd walked into that Manhattan rubber shop—he received it.

The world that had sneered at Charles Goodyear suddenly had at its disposal "vulcanized" rubber, a material that would make possible tires, gaskets, hot-water bottles, baseballs, balloons, blimps, bungee cords, tennis shoes, windshield wipers, waterbeds, pacifiers, garden hoses, conveyer belts, cable insulation, condoms, car bumpers, pencil erasers—in short, everything flexible and durable needed by a modern, industrial society. The man who had produced it, who had sacrificed everything to make it possible, expected to be rewarded.

When it became clear that Charles Goodyear really had solved rubber's problems, he suddenly found himself harassed with lawsuits. On one side, mercenary opportunists claimed *they* had actually discovered Goodyear's process and therefore deserved Goodyear's money. On the other, parasitic manufacturers wanted to squash his patents completely so that they could make rubber goods and not have to pay Goodyear a dime.

Dyspeptic and gout-ridden, often either flat on his back or hobbling about on crutches, Goodyear could have easily set himself up as the sole producer of vulcanized rubber, a monopoly that would have made him a multi-multi-millionaire. Instead, he licensed the right to manufacture rubber products to others and collected royalties on the goods sold. Goodyear didn't want to produce rubber; he wanted to develop new ways to use it. His only concern about the licensing arrangement was that outside firms might make flawed products, which would give rubber a bad name.

The licenses and royalties owed to Goodyear still should have made him rich, but Charles Goodyear was awful with money. He would take the income from one license, spend all of that and then some eagerly developing a new rubber item, then be forced to sell its manufacturing rights to another licensee to pay for his excess expenses. Manufacturers quickly saw that Goodyear operated from a position of perpetual weakness and took ruthless advantage of it. They wrangled agreements for pitifully small license fees and often defaulted on their equally meager royalty payments. Goodyear was usually too poor to hire lawyers to chase down the deadbeats, so he collected only a fraction of the money owed to him—which he of course put straight back into his experiments.

Goodyear was also kept poor by the expense of suing those who flagrantly stole his patented process and used it to make their own rubber products. The market was flooded with unlicensed goods from dozens of rogue manufacturers. One early thief had the secret of vulcanization sold to him by a bankrupt Goodyear licensee for a paltry $66, but even that effort would soon prove unnecessary. Vulcanization, it turned out, was easy to duplicate if one had money and facilities—which helps explain how easily Goodyear was cheated out of his patent rights abroad.

In England, some early samples of Goodyear rubber found their way into the hands of a British manufacturer, who guessed that the charred and foul-smelling substance combined heat and sulfur. He duplicated the process and patented it under his own name before Goodyear could file. The English government ignored Goodyear's protests, knowing that a British patent would save them millions in tariffs. In France, Goodyear's patent was voided because he had earlier sent a few vulcanized shoes to Paris. According to the French, that trivial action meant that Goodyear had legally given the invention to the French government, and France didn't have to pay Goodyear one cent to use it. Which they never did.

Goodyear knew his narrow-minded licensees had no interest in developing new products; they only wanted to make money selling items that were proven and popular. So Charles Goodyear assumed the burden and expense of research himself. Were it not for his efforts, rubber might still be used only for suspenders and raincoats. Charles Goodyear showed that rubber made excellent buttons, combs, canteens, harbor buoys, watch cases, and handles for tools and cutlery. To him we owe the rubber cushion, rubber band, rubber glove, and of course, the inflatable rubber life preserver.

One would think that Charles Goodyear would have at least been honored by the people for his tireless research and new rubber goods. Instead, they resented him. While the licensees skimped on paying Goodyear his fees, they were always careful to burn his "brand name" into their products, which now numbered in the hundreds. Charles Goodyear was delighted to see his name seared into his adored rubber, but it gave the public a false impression. Seeing GOODYEAR on everything from baby-bottle nipples to boot heels, they grumbled that he had become a wealthy, one-man monopoly. They would have been amazed to learn that Charles Goodyear was still being thrown into debtors' prisons.

Goodyear thought of himself as a good Christian, but his faith really was in rubber. He was always personally frugal and abstemious, but he was an incurable spend-thrift when promoting his cherished inert substance. He squandered $30,000 to build "Goodyear's Vulcanite Court" for the 1851 Great Exposition in London and another $50,000 for a similar display at the 1855 Exposition Universelle in Paris—no doubt the greatest sums he ever spent on anything in his life. Both exhibits boasted a suite of rooms in which everything—walls, doors, flooring, furniture, lamps, artwork, carpets, and draperies— was made of rubber. The Vulcanite Court at the Great Exposition occupied more space than all the other American exhibits combined.

The Vulcanite Court was the embodiment of Goodyear's "connected system of inventions," a glorious future world in which nearly everything would be made of rubber. From 1844 onward he devoted all of his energies to completing this "plan of improvement" before he died. Goodyear created rubber sails to drive ships, rubber "map carpets" that gave a geographic education while they muffled noise, rubber money that could be boiled clean and reused. Goodyear literally lived in a rubber universe. His business cards were made of rubber. He wore rubber vests, hats, and ties. His office door had a rubber nameplate, his official portrait was painted on rubber, his autobiography was printed on rubber tissue and bound between hard rubber covers, carved with scenes depicting a rubber harvest.

Still, all the positive thinking in the world could not counteract the bad luck and lack of capital that dogged Charles Goodyear. His long-suffering wife died at age forty-nine, an old, old woman. Goodyear, frail and sickly, knowing he was incapable of taking care of himself, quickly remarried. He then pawned his new wife's engagement ring to pay for more experiments. While in

Paris he was awarded the Cross of the Legion of Honor by Emperor Napoleon III—in debtors' prison.

Goodyear returned to America but found no peace or rest. Business and political interests, eager to prevent the renewal of Goodyear's patent, began a smear campaign portraying him as a fanatic who had been abundantly rewarded, wasted his money, and therefore didn't deserve any more. Goodyear's weakened health, always bad, declined precipitously.

In May of 1860 Goodyear learned that his daughter Cynthia was critically ill in Connecticut, and he set out from Washington to visit her. He stopped in New York, too feeble to continue or return home, when news reached him that Cynthia had died the previous day—the seventh of his twelve children to pass away before him. Goodyear spent his last month slowly dying in a Manhattan hotel room. He breathed his last on July 1, at age fifty-nine. The press either dismissed his passing in a sentence or two or failed to report it at all. *Scientific American* commented: "He spent his money like water, when he ought to have taken care of his family."

Charles Goodyear had never kept any books or memoranda to track his income. It was impossible to say how much money he'd made (or should have made) from vulcanized rubber. After his death, Goodyear's attorneys reckoned that his total profit for twenty-five years' work was $19,000. His son Charles Jr. went over the family finances and estimated that his father had died $191,000 in debt. Both calculations were brought before Congress in 1865, which was then considering the Goodyear patent extension. To the family's horror, Congress ignored their figures and instead favored the wild—and utterly base-less—accusations made by the rubber manufacturers, who declared that Goodyear had amassed a personal fortune of $50 to 75 million. Goodyear's attorneys pointed out that these accusations were being made by the same manufacturers who had spent years evading their license fees and pirating Goodyear's patents. Congress chose to ignore that, too. The patent extension was denied.

Joseph Holt, Commissioner of Patents, summed up the miserable life of Charles Goodyear as the price of vision. "Such in all times," he wrote, "has been the fate of the greatest spirits that have appeared in the arena of human discovery, and such will probably continue to be the doom of all whose stalwart strides carry them in advance of the race to which they belong."

The multibillion-dollar corporation that currently uses the Goodyear name has no connection to the Goodyear family. It was formed nearly forty years after Charles Goodyear died. He never saw a dime from it.

# 15

# The Most
# Wonderful Boy
# in the World

THE GAME OF "WHAT IF" IS MADDENING AND ULTIMATELY
fruitless, since we can never really know what might have
been. Still, it's hard not to feel cheated when one consid-
ers the intellect of William James Sidis, perhaps the most
brilliant mind of the twentieth century, who simply
refused to give humanity the benefit of his knowledge
because, frankly, humanity didn't deserve it.

Sidis was a child prodigy—some say the greatest who
ever lived—with an IQ estimated at 250 to 300 (Einstein's was a paltry 200). He was born to parents who
were gifted and driven. Both Boris Sidis and Sarah Man-
delbaum had fled poverty and persecution in the Ukraine,
and they had met in Boston when Boris first became

Sarah's tutor, then her husband. Sarah went on to become the first woman doctor to graduate from Boston University School of Medicine. Boris enrolled at Harvard, where he received his B.A. in a single year, magna cum laude. Harvard granted him a Ph.D. without a thesis or an oral examination—he was that brilliant. Sarah's pet name for him was "Dr. Science."

In 1898 Boris joined the staff of Manhattan's Pathological Institute, a pioneering hospital for the investigation and treatment of psychological disorders. At about the same time Boris and Sarah's first child, William, was born. When he was still in the womb his parents made several fateful decisions about his future. They agreed to rear him using new teaching techniques that Boris had developed, and they agreed to stress the attributes that they valued most: intellect, discipline, and hard work. William would be taught in an atmosphere of mutual respect, which to Boris and Sarah meant that their little boy would be treated as if he were an adult from the day he was born.

There's no question that Boris and Sarah loved William. Boris later wrote in his book *Philistine and Genius* (one of seventeen he had published in his lifetime) that he and his wife were always "reasonable and truthful and logical" with their son. But their reasonableness only operated within their belief that the best way to raise a child was to focus exclusively on intellectual education. "A baby is never too young to learn anything," Boris wrote. "Minds are built with use." Boris and Sarah felt that children trained to reason would have a bulwark against brutality, ignorance, and superstitious beliefs. It was never too early to begin "bending the minds of children in the right direction" so that they would grow up "rational."

For all their good intentions, Boris and Sarah failed to see that their own intellectualism had developed gradually and had been a matter of choice. William was not given those options. Both parents insisted that William was never forced to learn anything, yet he lived in an environment where it was impossible to escape the cerebral. Learning was honored in the Sidis household; ordinary, childlike behavior was not. William's bedtime stories were the Greek myths. Nothing colorful or cute was allowed in his crib; his first toys were alphabet and number blocks, books, maps, and a globe. Infant William ate at the table with his parents; no high chair was allowed. Both parents disapproved of baby talk and always spoke to William as they would their peers.

Hour after hour Boris and Sarah would form words with William's blocks and point to the objects they represented. They hoped to tap the "reserve energy" that Boris believed was inherent in the human brain. Apparently they did. William spoke his first word at six months. At eighteen months he was reading the *New York Times*. At two he was typing in both English and French. By age three, as a present to his father, William announced that he had taught himself Latin, and indeed he had.

William's astonishing feats of learning came at a price. His parents' program of treating William as an adult completely ignored the boy's undeveloped emotional and social needs. Both Boris and Sarah also disdained sports, so William had virtually no physical activity. His only recreation was reading.

For the first six years of his life, William was always either alone or in the company of adults. He had no siblings, no playmates, no friends his own age. Boris and

Sarah saw nothing wrong in this and would take him to parties where William would demonstrate his photographic memory and other remarkable abilities before their enraptured colleagues.

William's prodigious intellect developed at a blistering pace. At six he could read and speak at least eight languages and had worked out a formula to instantly name the day of the week of any date in history. At seven he passed the Harvard Medical School anatomy exam. By eight he had devised a profound new logarithmic table using a base of twelve and had written his own textbooks on astronomy, linguistics, and mathematics. He mastered trigonometry, geometry, and differential calculus by the age of ten, and he created his own universal language ("Vendergood") and wrote the constitution for a planned Utopia ("Hesperia") before he had reached puberty.

William entered the public school system in 1904 and rocketed from first to eighth grade in only seven months. Most of the time in school he was bored, unhappy, and lonely. William's only enjoyment came from learning something new—which he did instantly upon encountering it—and from engaging in intellectual discussions with his instructors. He shunned his fellow students and they shunned him.

William's seven months in grammar school made it clear to others—if not to William and his parents—that he had no notion of common courtesies. Interpersonal skills were of no interest to him and he had no qualms about straightforwardly expressing his opinions. William plugged his ears with his fingers to avoid hearing lessons that he had mastered years before. He told his teachers that he wanted to leave school because he "knew all they could teach him anyway." He wasn't being boastful, just honest. William couldn't understand that people might be offended by his behavior, and Boris and Sarah apparently felt no reason to tell him that humans are social animals as well as intellectual beings.

This was a critical piece of wisdom to be lacking, especially as William, now outside the Sidis family cocoon, was attracting press attention. Boris and Sarah did nothing to discourage the media. They were blind to the outcast they were creating and saw William's outstanding mental abilities as a justification of their educational theories and as an inspiration to other parents. William, in their minds, was something to be displayed because he was the best that a child could possibly be.

William, by contrast, hungered for privacy and hated the spotlight. At first he had enjoyed the adulation of adults, but now he was being judged on much more than his ability to quote Shakespeare or identify Latin declensions. He was unprepared for the jealous snipes that began to appear in print, or for the opinion, often expressed, that as a genius he was expected to deliver some wonderful discovery to humankind.

By the time William was eight he had passed the entrance exam for the Massachusetts Institute of Technology. He was instead sent to high school, where he completed the four-year curriculum in six weeks. "Why should I spend my time on things I know," he asked one professor, "when there are things I don't know?" At nine he applied to Harvard and was rejected only because of his youth. The same thing happened when he applied at age ten. But the following year the faculty gave in and accepted William Sidis as a "special student," thus making the eleven-year-old the youngest person ever to be enrolled at that university.

It was while he was still eleven, in January 1910, that William Sidis reached the apex of his brief scholastic career. Wearing the short pants of a grade-schooler, he delivered a two-hour lecture titled "Four-Dimensional Bodies" to the awestruck Harvard Mathematical Club. It was a brilliant triumph of a brilliant mind, and William Sidis instantly became a household name. Many publications praised "the most wonderful boy in the world" and the equally wonderful parents who had created him. Others had a decidedly different view. Several predicted a mental collapse for William. One quoted a doctor who feared that the prodigy might die of "overstudy."

William, through no fault of his own, had become controversial. He had been too smart for too long, and many were resentful of it. If, as his parents repeatedly insisted, William was no different from any other child, then why did he make every other "normal" boy and girl appear so backward? There was something threatening in this strange-mannered adolescent who was brainier than almost every adult he had encountered. The public, with the press as an eager accomplice, was itching to find fault in the boy genius, and his lack of social grace and blunt truthfulness were ideally suited to that purpose.

The engineered destruction of William Sidis was perhaps the first instance of America's twentieth-century tendency to deify a hero, then rip him to shreds. It was no different in degree from the savageries that toppled movie stars and sports celebrities of later generations. But this was the 1910s, there were no spokespersons to shield the targeted, and in any case the head on the public chopping block belonged to a painfully maladjusted fourteen-year-old boy. Boris and Sarah, who prided themselves on their knowledge of psychology, hadn't a clue.

Reporters followed William everywhere around campus, poking and prying, trying to learn any detail about him that might make juicy copy. They gleefully noted that the boy wonder had no interest in art or girls (in fact, he had taken a vow of celibacy), subsisted on a diet of crackers and dairy products, disliked flowers, music, and all sports, and had no concern for his personal appearance. They darkly suggested that he occasionally suffered "nervous prostration" from "too great mental exertion."

By now the Sidis family was running its own sanitarium, the Sidis Psychopathic Institute, in Portsmouth, New Hampshire. It was a first-of-its-kind operation, and its patients were among the richest neurotics in New England. Whenever William left Harvard during semester breaks, the press dutifully reported that his home was a place that treated the mentally ill. The public took the hint and believed William was on the verge of a breakdown.

Young William's politics also generated reams of sensational newsprint for the fourth estate. To the horror of his teachers, he had declared himself an atheist at the age of six and made no secret of it in the classroom. He had also inherited his parents' freethinking idealism and had developed a passion for radical socialism. The "disrespectful" public manner of William Sidis, so often criticized by others, stemmed from his sincere belief in individual liberty: the idea that people ought to be able to do as they please as long as their pleasure didn't hurt anyone else.

William Sidis graduated from Harvard cum laude in his class. He was a scholar in logic, philosophy, ancient and American history, economic and political theory, languages (he could learn one in a day), astronomy, anatomy, comparative philology and mythology, linguistics, mathematics, integral calculus, theoretical physics, and Euclidean geometry—and he was only sixteen years old. William Sidis was among the very, very few intellects in history to have mastered so many branches of human thought. When asked by the ever-present reporters about his future plans, he replied, "I have always hated crowds," and he explained that he intended to drop out of sight, retreat into his intellectual pursuits, and "seek happiness in my own way."

That, of course, would never be possible for William Sidis. He was lambasted in the press as "unnatural" and "an intolerable prig"—in short, he was being pilloried for not pledging his life to the society that mocked him. William received no emotional support from his parents, who were unwilling to concede that their educational theories had produced a flawed result.

Boris and Sarah, believing that what their happiness-seeking son really needed was a change of scene, sent him to Rice University in Houston, Texas, where he was hired to teach mathematics and geometry. At seventeen, he was the youngest professor in American history; yet another first for the boy wonder. He did not last long in the job. Sloppy and unsociable, he was constantly teased by the students—all older than him—and was made the subject of humiliating newspaper stories and jokes because he had truthfully admitted that he had never kissed a girl. According to one faculty member, "he was treated like a two-headed calf."

Back to Boston came William Sidis, this time to enroll at Harvard Law School. The browbeaten genius began expanding his involvement with leftist politics, claiming draft exemption as a conscientious objector and becoming a member of the Socialist Party. The Socialists were of course ecstatic to have a public figure like William as one of their members. They made certain he felt welcome and important.

On May 1, 1919, the most wonderful boy in the world—who had quit law school the previous spring— was thrown into jail on the charge of "incitement to riot." He had been given a red flag to carry at the head of a march of Socialists through the streets of Roxbury. The protest quickly degenerated into a brawl, as police and military veterans attacked the demonstrators with billy clubs, bats, and whatever else they could grab. William was beaten and thrown into the Roxbury lockup with over a hundred others.

William Sidis, passionate and sincere, had been used by the Socialists. Now he was used once again by his parents. Boris pulled strings to free him from jail, but he left the threat of reimprisonment open as a way of keeping William in line. Demoralized and frightened, William was whisked away to Portsmouth and then to California by Boris and Sarah, who kept him under tight control for two years while they attempted to reprogram their wayward genius.

William later described these years in the third person, remembering that he had been "kept under various kinds of mental torture, consisting of being scolded and

nagged at . . . for an average of six to eight hours a day."
Sometimes, he recalled, this scolding was administered
while he was loaded with tranquilizers, or after being
waked out of a sound sleep. "And the threat of being
transferred to a regular insane asylum was held up in
front of him constantly, with detailed descriptions of the
tortures practiced there, as well as of the simple legal
process by which he could be committed to such a place."
By the time Boris and Sarah allowed William to leave in
late 1921, he was "scared of his own shadow."

William Sidis had had enough. He moved to New York,
where he made one last contribution to advanced
thought, a major work of theoretical physics titled *The
Animate and the Inanimate*. In it he described his doctrine
of "the reversibility of the universe," which questioned
the Second Law of Thermodynamics and predicted the
existence of antimatter and black holes. It was a ground-
breaking work, written almost two decades before Sub-
rahmanyan Chandrasekhar published *Study of Stellar
Structure*, which is usually recognized as the first book to
tackle such impenetrable subjects.

Sidis wrote *The Animate and the Inanimate* when he
was twenty-four. It was completely ignored by both the
academic community and the press, which was more
interested in printing stories such as FORMER RICE
INSTRUCTOR WHO DEFAMED HOUSTON GIRLS IS NOW A RED
FLAGGER. William Sidis simply shut down. His remarkable mind was as sharp as ever, but he refused to use it.
The human race, which ridiculed Sidis as a freak while
demanding that he live up to his potential, was not worth
his effort.

Sidis spent the remainder of his life as anonymously as possible, employed as an adding-machine operator in a series of meaningless jobs. When his co-workers would tease him about his dress or grooming, or when his employers would discover his abilities and demand that he take a more responsible position, he would quit. He lived in rooming houses and never made more than $25 a week. He was, in the opinion of those who knew him, happier than he had ever been in his life.

William Sidis died at forty-six of a brain hemorrhage. To the end, he refused to have anything to do with the academic and intellectual world, or with the parents who had perverted his life. He was buried next to his father, whose funeral William Sidis did not attend.

# 16

# Sex and Anarchy

THE THREE-RING CIRCUS OF PSEUDOSCIENCE HAS PRODUCED its share of charlatans and crackpots, but rarely has it manifested a character more difficult to label than Wilhelm Reich. That would have pleased him; he hated labels. He also hated injustice, closed minds, "mechanistic thinking," and shallow breathing. He called himself a natural scientist and dedicated his life to improving the lot of humankind, which repaid his efforts with fear and derision. Toward the end, he believed that he could control the weather and that his father was a space alien.

There's little doubt that Reich was half-mad in his later years. But his body of work is often dismissed based on his messy exit, and that is unfair. Kepler, Planck, and Einstein, among others, had brilliant minds that eventually went astray. If we do not judge Newton on his mysticism or Jung on his dabblings in alchemy, we should not judge Reich on his flying saucer theories—although the people who ordered his books burned, trashed his laboratory, and threw him into a federal penitentiary where he would eventually die no doubt wish that we would.

Wilhelm Reich was born in Austria in 1897. By the age of twenty-one he had survived the trench warfare of World War I and the suicides of his mother and father, who wanted Wilhelm to use their life insurance money to go to college. These tragic events fired him with loathing for authority and profit, yet they also fostered in him a passionate desire to heal the wounded human soul. He would walk these paths, dark and light, for the rest of his life.

Reich attended medical school in Vienna and devoted his energies to the new field of psychiatry. His quick mind rapidly propelled him into the directorship of the Seminar for Psychoanalytic Therapy, at that time the world center for psychoanalyst training. His theories were daring, his technique bold. Over the next dozen years he would author several major books on human sexuality and his name would be advanced as a candidate for a Nobel Prize.

Reich grew up in a world where sex was regarded as a biological act, pleasurable for a man, dutiful for a woman, and always somehow improper. Yet as he practiced psychoanalysis, Reich was disturbed to discover that most of his patients were emotionally deadened, even those who led active sex lives. Reich saw a connection and theorized that people didn't truly know how to make love, which he felt was necessary for emotional and physical well-being. To put it bluntly, people needed good orgasms to be happy. And to have good orgasms, Reich believed, people needed intelligent sex education, an appreciation for gentleness and openness in sexual intercourse, and freer sexuality in general. This is fodder for daytime talk shows today, but it was taboo territory during Reich's lifetime.

Reich was doubly threatening because he combined his revolutionary views of sexuality with politics. Good sex, he argued, was politically liberating and made people more independent and less inclined to follow orders mindlessly. In 1929 he opened sex hygiene clinics for young people in Vienna; in the 1930s he was in Berlin advocating birth control and publishing sex education pamphlets for adolescents. For this pioneering social work he was kicked out of one European country after another, from Austria to Germany to Denmark to Sweden to Norway, before he was finally invited to immigrate to America in 1939.

Reich's move to the United States did not lessen his contempt for the mainstream, and in the mid-1940s he moved his laboratory from New York City to an abandoned farm outside the small town of Rangeley, Maine. He dubbed the farm "Orgonon." There he surrounded himself with the best equipment he could afford (nearly all his research was funded out of his own pocket) and a small company of dedicated researchers, doctors, and psychiatrists. They called themselves "medical orgonomists" and were loyal to Reich, who rarely tolerated disagreement. Those who failed to understand his concepts were kicked out. As a result, Reich gradually became surrounded by a small circle of awestruck followers, rather than a spectrum of intellectually challenging colleagues. This would serve him poorly in the difficult years to come.

Reich continued to champion the cause of healthy sex. His writings promoted sexual (and political) equality for women, legalized abortion, contraceptives for teen-agers, tolerance for homosexuality, and sex education in the schools and in the mass media. His mission, as he saw it, was "to break through the barrier which separates the public from its own private life." When asked why he was "obsessed with sex" he always answered that some-thing so important to human happiness should never be shunned, particularly by science.

*Harper's Magazine* did not see it that way. It published an article in April 1947 titled "The New Cult of Sex and Anarchy," in which uneasy psychiatrists and psychoana-lysts called Reich dangerous and schizophrenic. In hind-sight, it's difficult to see what was dangerous about someone who championed commonsense sexual responsi-bility; stressed that sexual satisfaction was impossible unless both partners shared mature, emotional love; scorned "freedom peddlers" who promised instant gratification without accountability; detested pornography or anything that cheapened human sexuality; and believed that a sexually educated and mature society would have fewer neuroses, no need for prostitution, no venereal dis-ease, and no sexual violence. But in 1947 Reich's views were years ahead of their time. The public read of his advo-cacy of nudity in the home, masturbation, and liberal divorce laws and branded him a pornographer, a "sex fiend," and a mastermind of orgies—concepts utterly alien to his theories of love-based, one-on-one relationships.

Reich ignored the criticism and continued his work. He also continued to speak out for what he believed in, which included the abolishment of capitalism, Western medicine, and orthodox psychiatry, all of which he saw as obstacles to human health. Reich never understood the value of good public relations. He ridiculed those who feared new discoveries and wrote frequently of the economic and political collusion among America's major drug companies, the medical establishment, and federal regulatory agencies.

These opinions did not sit well with America's businessmen, doctors, and politicians. Wilhelm Reich, they told themselves, was a kook with credentials, an author of books with dangerous ideas. Now that he was attracting the interest of the mass media, it would be best if some way could be found to shut him down.

Most of the work at Orgonon centered around "orgone," the biophysical "life energy" that Reich felt fueled the human libido and immune system. Orgone had nothing to do with why Wilhelm Reich would be thrown into jail to die. But, unlike his ideas, orgone led to something tangible—a therapeutic device. And that was something that could be snared through legalistic mechanisms and used to silence Wilhelm Reich.

Reich believed that orgone was present in everything natural and that all living things drew energy from it. Consequently, people suffering from degenerative diseases—most notably cancer—could strengthen their bodies' immune systems if they could get more orgone.

Since orgone was in the air, Reich built "orgone accumulators"—simple wood boxes lined with sheet metal—that trapped orgone much as a greenhouse traps heat. Patients would sit in these narrow boxes—each roughly the size of a phone booth—and absorb orgone until they were "charged." The treatment was physically harmless, with roots in natural healing. It was, to all appearances, hogwash. Yet a number of terminally ill cancer patients who sat in Reich's boxes reported favorable results. Reich proudly wrote that orgone was useful as a cancer therapy.

That was what Reich's opponents had been waiting for. Ever since the *Harper's Magazine* article the FDA had been quietly gathering information about Reich and his "orgasm boxes," much of it from the American Medical Association and the American Psychiatric Association (who considered Reich an embarrassing eccentric) as well as the people of Rangeley (who believed that Orgonon was a front for a "sex cult"). Now they lowered the boom.

The FDA filed an injunction accusing Reich of violating the Federal Pure Food and Drug Act by peddling a fraudulent cancer cure. True to his contempt for government bureaucracies, Reich refused to appear in court to contest the charges. That was a bad move. The injunction was full of misrepresentations and falsehoods; Reich very likely could have had it thrown out. Nevertheless, he refused to defend himself. What mattered, he said, was not what people thought of him but what he did. He failed to understand that what certain people thought of him—in particular the federal judge presiding over the case—mattered a great deal. So while Reich remained at Orgonon with his loyal assistants, the injunction went through uncontested and the judge ordered that all of Reich's orgone accumulators be recalled and destroyed.

In fairness to the FDA, cancer treatments did have a long and unsavory history of quackery. It was understandable that they would take an extremely dim view of anyone who suggested that sitting in a box might help a patient with leukemia or a malignant tumor. But the court order that the FDA engineered went much further than that of a bureaucratic watchdog protecting the nation's afflicted. It ordered that all of Reich's books be banned from sale or distribution and that everything published by Reich in English—including books that merely contained the words *cancer* or *blood*—be crated, shipped to the nearest federal incinerator, and burned. Works such as *The Mass Psychology of Fascism, Character Analysis,* and *The Sexual Revolution* were thus to be delivered to the flames simply because Reich was their author.

The parallels to Nazi Germany—which twenty years earlier had also ordered Reich's books to be burned—were lost on the federal court. But they were not lost on Reich and his supporters, who refused to obey the judge's order. The orgone accumulators were not destroyed, the books remained in print and out of the federal bonfire.

Reich's natural distrust of authority now boiled into paranoia. He insisted that the FDA men were "stooges" working in collusion with Soviet Russia, and no one was around to persuade him otherwise. His colleagues in medicine, psychiatry, and psychology ignored his plight; many practitioners quietly agreed that Reich deserved to be chastised. He had long since isolated himself from anyone with credentials and common sense. His band of loyal orgonomists—who now carried guns at Orgonon—was more ideological than practical. On more than one occasion Reich fired his shotgun into the air to ward off FDA agents. "I was ready to die," Reich later said, rather than obey the injunction. He had his burial plot prepared in anticipation of a bloody showdown.

It never came to that. Oblivious to Reich's dramatic posturing, the wheels of American justice rolled forward. Reich was charged with criminal contempt for refusing to obey the judge's order, arrested when he left the compound, and brought to trial in federal court in May 1956.

Stubborn and proud, Reich insisted on carrying out his own defense. What followed was the pathetic spectacle of a formerly brilliant man, now only partially lucid, trying to refute charges that were fundamentally unjust but perfectly legal. The *Portland Press Herald* called the resulting show "one of the most colorful trials in many months."

Reich lashed out at his accusers, claiming that the government had no right to persecute him for purely scientific experiments that had harmed no one. He argued that the court lacked jurisdiction over natural science, that scientific inquiry should be free from political interference, that "orgone energy has a right to flourish," and that if lawyers and politicians were allowed to decide what was right and wrong, the future of scientific research was "gone to the dogs."

In his closing arguments, the prosecutor remarked that this was "probably the first time in the annals of jurisprudence that the government has presented a case only to have the defendants come in and say they did it." It was true. Reich freely admitted that he had violated the court's injunction, that it had to be violated, and that he "would do it again under the same circumstances." Perhaps out of compassion, the judge forbid any testimony as to what those "circumstances" were (Reich believed that the earth was about to be attacked by flying saucers). The only issue on trial, he said, was whether or not Reich had violated the injunction. The verdict on that issue was never in doubt.

Reich's high-minded rhetoric failed to impress a jury of his peers, who found him guilty after only twenty minutes of deliberation. On May 25, 1956, he was fined $10,000 (a considerable sum in those days) and sentenced to two years in a federal penitentiary. The severity of the sentence surprised even those who had dismissed Reich as a crackpot. Reich was a heavy smoker and had a bad heart, which a prolonged jail term could only weaken. After eight months in prison, two days before his parole hearing, he was found dead on the floor of his cell. He was sixty.

Agents of the FDA entered Orgonon and destroyed every orgone accumulator they could find. Reich's German-language texts were banned from distribution and sale. All his English-language books were burned in federal incinerators. New editions of Reich's works would not be published until the 1970s.

Reich's loyal followers rallied around their martyred leader, which only made things worse. They howled that Reich had been poisoned in prison, silenced because his space-alien conspiracy theories were true. This sideshow obscured the larger truth, that Reich's civil rights and freedom of speech had been crushed simply because he had said and written things that conflicted with the political, economic, and moral interests of America's governing class.

Wilhelm Reich had often remarked that he didn't care if he were recognized in his own lifetime. He felt confident that his theories would be appreciated by future generations, and that was enough for him. "Civilization has not been yet," he once wrote.

Apparently not. Sexual neuroses still plague us, and Wilhelm Reich's followers seem content to build orgone accumulators and debate his theory of weather control.

# 17

# A Woman of the People

To outsiders they were known as the Paiute, a loose confederation of small tribes that roamed the wind-blown Great Basin of western Nevada. Among themselves they were Numa, the People, and they spent most of their nomadic existence gathering roots and seeds for food and harvesting bulrushes to make the baskets, clothing, and huts that constituted their meager possessions.

Thocmetony, whose name meant "shellflower," was the daughter of Winnemucca, the eldest son of Truckee, the head chief of the Paiute tribes. She was born most likely in 1844. The world into which she arrived had followed its predictable customs as long as any of the People could remember, generation after generation.

Whites also arrived in the Great Basin in 1844. Chief Truckee (whose name meant "very good") acted as one of their guides. He believed in peace and cooperation, and he believed the Indians and the white people were brothers.

When gold was discovered in California, prospectors by the tens of thousands crossed the Great Basin, killing animals, raiding the Numa's precious stocks of food, and often shooting Indians on sight. White settlers came soon afterward, fencing off the meadows and other prime land for their livestock. Some of the Paiute fought back, but Truckee counseled understanding. He had been to California, had seen the towns that harbored thousands of whites, and knew of lands to the east that harbored millions more. He told the Numa that the only way they could survive was to keep peace with the settlers.

As part of this plan, Truckee sent Thocmetony to California to be taught the ways of the white people. She was given the biblical name Sarah and the last name of her father. As Sarah Winnemucca she learned to use tables and chairs, cups and plates, and to sleep in a bed. She also learned to speak English and Spanish, for Sarah was a bright girl with a natural affinity for learning languages.

In the Great Basin white settlers continued to overrun the land and shoot Indians who opposed them. Epidemics of cholera, pneumonia, and tuberculosis devastated the natives, who had no natural immunity. Still, Truckee preached peace and cooperation. His wishes prevailed while he lived, for Truckee was a powerful man, respected by all. The settlers saw the Paiute as an intelligent, "docile" people and agreed to a treaty of friendship. In California, Sarah was moved into the home of a local military commander, William Ormsby, where she learned to read, write, and to dress like a white woman. She was only fifteen, but already she possessed knowledge and skills far beyond those of most Southwestern Indians.

The years of peace ended in 1859, when huge deposits of silver ore were discovered in the mountains that bordered the Great Basin. New whites arrived who cared nothing for treaties and cooperation. The pine forests were cut for mine timbers, more meadows were fenced off, and the fragile land could no longer support all of the people who lived on it. The Indians were hungry.

Truckee died later that year. Winnemucca became head chief of the Paiute, and he was weak. The people—on the brink of starvation—no longer wanted peace with the whites. Already a strong-willed young woman, Sarah counseled otherwise. She urged the Numa to follow the teachings of her grandfather. Their only hope, she said, lay in education and in friendship with the settlers. But although Sarah was the daughter of the head chief, her arguments carried little weight. In the mountains surrounding the Great Basin, the Paiute tribes gathered for war.

Sarah returned to California for more education, this time in a convent school run by nuns. She hoped to become proficient in grammar, geography, philosophy, and arithmetic so that she could return to teach her people what she had learned. Her dreams were shattered when she was expelled after only three weeks. The school's well-to-do patrons—outraged that their children were associating with an Indian—had threatened to withdraw their financial support if Sarah was allowed to stay.

The war that Sarah feared broke out in 1860, and the fighting went surprisingly well for the Numa, at least at the start. The white volunteers, led by Sarah's former mentor, William Ormsby, arrogantly refused the Paiute's repeated truce offers. Ormsby led his men headlong into a trap; they were slaughtered. Triumph for the Numa turned to disaster, however, when army troops from California arrived and drove the Paiute completely out of the Great Basin. When a truce was arranged a year later, Sarah's people found that the soldiers had built a fort on their land. The Paiute were given a section of the Basin around Pyramid Lake as their reservation. They were told that their nomadic way of life was over. So were their days of self-sufficiency. The Numa, though they didn't yet realize it, had become wards of the United States government.

Cold winters followed. The unscrupulous agent who ran the Pyramid Lake reservation sold the supplies earmarked for the Indians and pocketed the money for himself. Although there was already too little land to provide food for the Paiute, the agent sold much of what was left to the railroads, who in turn sold it to white settlers at a considerable profit. The agent turned his back—usually for a bribe—while white squatters stole Indian forage, timber, and livestock. Living in shacks that barely provided protection from the weather, the Paiute had to sift through the garbage dumps of the whites for food. They stood outside the mine shafts and begged the men for leftovers from their lunch pails. Half-starved Indians were reported living on undigested barley that they washed out of horse manure.

Chief Winnemucca, unwilling to fight, spent most of his time with Paiute tribes in Oregon. Other chiefs followed his example, leading their people off the reservation and into the surrounding mountains where they at least had a slim chance of finding food. Sarah, however, was stubbornly determined to stick it out. Although she was powerless, she remained on the reservation and did what she could to help her tribe. To survive, she washed the clothes of the hated agent. He paid her in flour that was supposed to have been given to the Numa.

Fortune smiled on Sarah Winnemucca, however wanly, in 1867. Overcome with grief at the poverty and degradation of her people, she delivered an impassioned plea to the local army commander recounting the inhumane abuses the Numa had suffered. Although Sarah's words came from the heart and not from calculation, it turned out to be a politically savvy move. At that moment the army and the Bureau of Indian Affairs were squabbling over control of the western tribes, and while the army was powerless on the reservation, the local commander was empathetic. Sarah and her people were taken north and provided protection from the whites, by the whites, at Fort McDermitt. They had become welfare cases and had surrendered their freedom, but they were fed and clothed and were free to follow their customs.

Sarah and her people lived at the fort for three years, their numbers swelling to nine hundred as other Paiute bands arrived. Sarah became the fort's interpreter and grew in status among her people, who credited her with saving their lives. She dressed like a white woman and began socializing with the fort's officers.

In Washington the Bureau of Indian Affairs took note of what the army had done and demanded an end to it. Well-fed Indians were spoiled Indians, it argued. The army replied that well-fed Indians were also peaceful Indians, but the bureau seemed deaf to that reasoning. Indians, it declared, should be on reservations, learning to farm and to become productive members of society—a view that Sarah Winnemucca agreed with. What the bureau wasn't saying was that removing Indians from reservations took money away from the bureau, whose great holdings of cheap land and control of government provisions were lucrative sources of graft for those in power. The Paiute at Fort McDermitt were ordered back onto the Pyramid Lake reservation. They wouldn't benefit from the move, but that wasn't the point.

The Numa refused to go. Instead, they spent years wandering the remote hills and valleys of northern Nevada and southeastern Oregon, fearing both the settlers and the slow death of the reservations. The army was forbidden to assist them, and Indians who stole cattle were shot. Sarah still believed that their only hope lay in civilization, and when a new reservation opened in Oregon, managed by an honest agent, she persuaded her people to follow her there. The agent was tough, but fair, and the Numa were put to work growing crops, learning trades, and building what Sarah had always dreamed of, a school where she could teach the Paiute children.

This did not go over well with the reservation's white neighbors, who coveted the Indian land. They sent a letter of complaint to the Bureau of Indian Affairs, and the bureau obligingly gave the western end of the reservation to the whites. They also replaced the honest agent with a corrupt local storekeeper who had nothing but contempt for the Paiute. Once again the Indians were starved, the work programs ended, and Sarah's school was closed. When she complained as she had at Pyramid Lake, Sarah was banished from the reservation as a troublemaker.

Sarah had suffered enough. She took a job as a maid in a private home, hoping to save enough money to break free from her past and start her own life. She was young, educated, and obviously attractive to white men, several of whom had already proposed marriage. But the Numa could not let her go. Desperate for food, with their only alternative a war that they knew would destroy them, the people secretly brought Sarah back to the reservation and asked her to go to Washington to plead their case directly to the president. They gave her all the money they had, $29.25.

It was an impossible task but Sarah shouldered it, as she had so much else in her life, because her people had no one else to turn to. True to form, her best efforts were betrayed by events. The war broke out before she had even reached the Idaho border. While there, Sarah learned that her father, who still refused to fight, had been captured by the Indian rebels. The army offered a $500 reward to anyone who would rescue him, but no one—Indian or white—would attempt the suicidal mission. Sarah did. She snuck into the enemy camp and spirited away not only her father but almost a hundred other Paiute followers who had also been captured. For the next three months she worked on the front lines of the war, acting as official interpreter for the army, reading signal fires, pinpointing enemy locations, and generally helping to lead the fight against fellow Indians because she knew that her people had to cooperate with the whites or die.

When the fighting ended, Chief Winnemucca called his people together and told them of his daughter's courage, noting that she had fought in battle while he had not. "Now," he said, "hereafter we will look on her as our chieftain, for none of us are worthy of being chief but her." Thus in 1877 the reigns of power passed to Sarah Winnemucca, the only woman ever to govern the Paiute.

It was a singular honor, but it amounted to little. In a confederacy as loosely knit as the Paiute, there were always other chiefs to whom dissidents could turn. Although Sarah traveled from village to village, trying to bring the scattered Paiute together, most resisted her pleas to return to a promised resettlement on a reservation in the Great Basin. Only one band of Paiute agreed to follow her. They soon regretted it, for Sarah was again betrayed.

Unknown to Sarah, the Bureau of Indian Affairs had decided that the last place it wanted the Paiute was back in the Great Basin, which was rapidly being settled by whites. Instead of heading south to Nevada, Sarah and her people were given three days' notice before being forcibly marched 350 miles over two mountain ranges, in the dead of winter, to a desolate, overcrowded reservation in Yakima City, Washington. The Paiute condemned Sarah for leading them into a trap; the army officers were sympathetic but would not disobey their orders. Sarah forced herself to cooperate, knowing that rebellion would only bring worse hardships.

What Sarah and her people suffered over the next five years was perhaps no more or less awful than the atrocities inflicted on other tribes, but the misery of those tribes went unrecorded. The Numa had Sarah, who was literate, had a good memory, and possessed the ability to write in the language of her persecutors. What Sarah witnessed became chapters in *Life Among the Paiute,* the first book written by a Native American in the English language.

The march to Yakima City was made without food and winter clothing. It took over a month, with the Paiute forced to camp in the snow with only canvas tents for shelter. Those who died were left on the open ground to be devoured by wolves.

When the rag-clad survivors stumbled into the Yakima City reservation in early February, its agent claimed that he hadn't been notified of their arrival. There was no food for the Paiute, no wood to build fires to keep them warm. A long shed, erected in one day, became their only shelter against the brutal winter. To make matters worse, the Yakima tribe, which already lived on the reservation, were historically enemies of the Paiute. They promptly stole what little their new neighbors had brought with them. Fifty-eight Paiute died that first winter, thirty of them children. Their bodies were thrown into the river because graves could not be dug in the frozen ground.

Supplies for the Paiute didn't arrive until May, and those that came were woefully inadequate. The people continued to die. Sarah once again emerged in a position of authority as the reservation interpreter and once again opened a school for the Paiute children. In time, her devotion won the admiration and loyalty of her people, who forgave her for leading them into what was the worst hellhole of their lives. Where else could they go? The Paiute who had remained free were shot on sight, or tortured and then murdered, by whites who wanted to possess the land. At least on the overcrowded reservation the people were together and could work toward a better future. That, at any rate, was how Sarah saw it.

In late 1879, Sarah's $500 reward money finally arrived. Suddenly she had the power that money could bring, and she used it to travel to San Francisco and rent a hall to deliver a series of lectures. Only Sarah possessed the necessary skills and familiarity with white customs to pull off something so audacious. "If your people will help us ... I will promise to educate my people and make them law-abiding citizens of the United States," she told her audiences, who were touched by her heartbreaking descriptions of the cruelties the Paiute had suffered. Sarah Winnemucca was a hit. Buoyed by her success, she promised to take her lectures east. "I will expose all the rascals. I will save nobody. My mouth shall not be sealed."

Alarmed at Sarah's popularity, the Bureau of Indian Affairs grandly offered to pay her way to Washington, where she was promised an audience with the president. When she arrived, the bureau deliberately kept her busy sight-seeing, giving her few opportunities to talk to reporters. She did get to meet the president—literally— but he left the room before she had a chance to say a word. And when she expressed a desire to lecture, the secretary of the interior bluntly told her that it would not be permitted, as she had made her trip at the government's expense.

Sarah was sent back west with three written promises from the secretary: tents to shelter all the Paiute under her care; 160 acres of ancestral land for the head of each Paiute family; and freedom for the Paiute at Yakima City. None of these promises was kept.

With this betrayal, Sarah at last understood that cooperation with whites in government was pointless. But she still believed that the white people were decent. Rather than fight or flee, Sarah decided to continue the lecturing she'd begun in San Francisco. She took a job in Vancouver as an interpreter, and when she had saved enough money she again headed east, this time paying her own way, to tell her story.

Sarah prudently chose Boston, the center of white culture, not government, as her destination. She proved as popular there as she had been in San Francisco, and as the months passed she began to give talks in other cities as well: New York, Baltimore, Philadelphia. Audiences wept and cheered. Wherever she went, she circulated a petition to Congress that would set the Paiute in Yakima City free and give her people the ancestral land promised by the secretary of the interior. The lectures were free, but she accepted donations that would fund her ultimate dream, a school for the Paiute that would offer practical education while preserving their native language and culture. She also sold copies of her book, which was popular with the intelligentsia if not the general public.

Outraged, the Bureau of Indian Affairs fought back. No Indian woman was going to bust up their cash cow without a fight. Since they couldn't disprove Sarah's charges, they resorted to mudslinging. Sarah was branded a tool in the army's struggle to regain control of Indian affairs. She was labeled a drunk, "wholly unreliable," and "notorious for her untruthfulness." Plumbing the depths, the bureau noted that Sarah enjoyed the company of white men and leveled the wholly fabricated charge that she had been a prostitute in a Nevada whorehouse. (The bureau was apparently unaware that Paiute girls were forbidden even to talk to any man except their fathers and brothers.) Sarah fought back, adding an appendix to her book with over two dozen letters from prominent people attesting to her bravery, cooperation, and spotless moral character.

The bureau's campaign of slander backfired, rallying public sympathy to Sarah and her cause. Her petition overflowed with signatures, the donation money poured in. A little over a year after her arrival in Boston, the Senate passed a bill that gave the Yakima City Paiute their freedom and their promised ancestral lands. The bureau told Sarah that the army had cleared the old Pyramid Lake reservation of white trespassers and urged her to return and lead her people there.

A cynic would raise an eyebrow at this point and express serious doubts about the sincerity of Washington's bureaucrats, noting that their sudden generosity sounded less like beneficence and more like an attempt to get Sarah back west of the Rockies and out of the public eye. Sarah, however, was not a cynic, and in the summer of 1884 she joyfully gathered together her savings and headed off to Nevada, to the reservation she had left so long ago, heady with the prospects of her people's happiness and of finally building her school with the money she had earned by speaking and writing the truth.

Disaster followed, swift and relentless. First, Sarah was robbed of most of her money on the train before she reached Nevada. Then she learned that her brother was about to be thrown into jail for debt; the rest of her money went to him. Then the agent at Pyramid Lake showed how much weight a senate bill carried on an Indian reservation—he flatly refused to acknowledge it. The school would not be built and Sarah would not be hired as a teacher. She was broke, and when she wired Boston for her share of the profits from her book sales, she got back fifty dollars.

Meanwhile, the people had returned to Pyramid Lake, expecting a place of security and anticipating the ancestral land promised to them by the Senate. They got neither. The army had, in fact, cleared the reservation of white squatters, but then the bureau ordered the army to leave. As soon as they did, the white squatters returned. The ancestral land was just another empty promise.

Ironically, the only Paiute who got his 160 acres was Sarah's deadbeat brother. It was given to him by California senator Leland Stanford, who had heard of the Winnemucca family's woes. Sarah decided to open her cherished school on her brother's land and once again launched a fund-raising lecture tour, this time across California and Nevada. She ran the school successfully for a year, then calamity again overwhelmed her. Neighboring white farmers, coveting the Winnemucca land, cut off its irrigation water. Sarah's brother was forced to sell his crops at below-market prices, leaving no money to continue the school.

After thirty years of being humiliated, belittled, shifted from place to place, and treated as less than human, Sarah began to break down physically. Rheumatism, neuralgia, then tuberculosis assailed her. Still, she preached the doctrine of hard work and forgiveness to her people and continued to stress the value of education. "A few years ago you owned this great country," she wrote to the Paiute of California. "Today the white man owns it all and you own nothing. Do you know what did it? Education...."

That, and the will to use it ruthlessly.

Sarah Winnemucca died in obscurity at the age of forty-seven.

# 18

# *Irreconcilable Differences*

Aｍｅʀｉｃᴀ'ѕ ꜰɪʀѕᴛ ᴡᴏʀᴋɪɴɢ-ᴄʟᴀѕѕ ʀᴇᴠᴏʟᴛ ᴡᴀѕ ѕᴘᴇᴀʀʜᴇᴀᴅᴇᴅ by a labor union called the Industrial Workers of the World. The IWW is almost forgotten now, but at its peak in the early twentieth century it boasted a hundred thousand members and struck fear in corporate boardrooms across the country. It offered hope to the castoffs of American industrialism—the unskilled, the uneducated, the poor, the powerless—and its loyal members defended their "one big union" faithfully, often to the death.

Wesley Everest was one of the faithful. He was a lumberjack on Washington's Olympic Peninsula and he knew—as did every other "Wob" and "Wobbly"—the stories of those who had died for the IWW cause. One was Joel Hagglund, who had been executed by a firing squad allegedly on the orders of Utah's copper mining kings. Another was Frank Little, a Montana Wob organizer, who had been dragged behind a car until his skin was scraped off. To Everest these men were distant, mythic figures, enshrined in memorial portraits that hung in every IWW union hall. He could not have known that he was fated to complete the troika of martyrs.

Wobblies were radical and proud of it. They believed that bosses were parasites who lived off the labor of people who actually produced the wealth. The IWW's ultimate goal was to topple upper management from power in every industry and to abolish wage labor altogether. "There can be no peace," began its constitution, "so long as hunger and want are found among millions of working people and the few, who make up the employing class, have all the good things of life."

The Wobs were driven to their militancy by the generally terrible working conditions of the early twentieth century. The lumber mills and camps of the Pacific Northwest were no exception to the norm. Mill laborers, usually men with families, could barely make ends meet on their wages for a twelve-hour day. When injury struck, as it often did in the field or the dangerous mills, it was left to fellow workers and townspeople to save the family from starvation and pay for medical expenses. The lumber companies contributed nothing.

Men in the logging camps made better money than the mill hands, but they suffered for it. They were nicknamed "timber beasts"—a virtual human subspecies in the eyes of employers—and worked ten- or twelve-hour days, ate rotting food, and lived in crowded shacks where they slept on wood pallets. Loggers who wanted a mattress or blanket had to carry bedrolls on their backs from camp to camp, usually infested with bedbugs and lice. Disease and crippling injuries were constant companions, and the logging camps provided no place to wash or to dry the loggers' dripping, filthy clothes during the long rainy season. "The sweaty, steamy odors of a bunkhouse at night," wrote economist Rexford Tugwell, "would asphyxiate the uninitiated."

Into this pit of misery stepped the Wobblies, telling the loggers and mill hands to stand up and stick it to their bosses. The union gave formerly powerless men a sense of self-respect and hope. Soon lumberjacks, Wesley Everest among them, were gathering in dusty halls to sing union songs and plan strikes, slowdowns, and sabotage. River crews fought Wob pickets. Tough mill foremen threw Wob organizers into log ponds. Even tougher camp foremen busted jaws with beefy fists and cracked skulls with axe handles. It took nerve to be a Wobbly, but as desperate men they had nothing to lose. They were unwilling to compromise, and their scorching rhetoric made them "red-flag anarchists" in the eyes of the lumber operators and, unfortunately, the public.

One hotbed of IWW activity was Centralia, Washington, a logging town of some seven thousand filled with lumberjacks and sawmill workers and, more important, Wobblies and American Legionnaires.

As the Wobblies represented labor, the American Legion represented the business class. While the Wobs preached economic and social revolution, the Legionnaires backed what was then called "Americanism," a blend of flag-waving nativism and laissez-faire capitalism. Each side saw itself as patriotic and the other as a force of evil that would lead to the downfall of America. In short, they hated each other.

The Legion particularly hated the Wobblies because of the IWW's opposition to World War I. Wobbly literature had denounced warfare and militarism as activities that slaughtered the working class while lining the pockets of politicians and industrialists. When America entered the conflict in 1917, war fervor set off mass beatings and banishings of Wobblies nationwide. Patriotic zealots accused IWW strikers of being traitorous agents of the German kaiser, of being "Imperial Wilhelm's Warriors." A citizen from Tulsa, Oklahoma, told one reporter, "The first step in the whipping of Germany is to strangle the IWW's. Don't scotch 'em—kill 'em dead."

Anti-Wobbly hysteria did not abate when the war ended; it intensified. The flames of fear and hate were fanned by the timber barons and the newspapers that served their interests. Armed men, it was written, would be needed to preserve order in the Pacific Northwest from the "Bolshevik" Wobblies. The Legionnaires were the obvious choice to be those armed men. In 1919, the Legion's state headquarters made it official when it asked that every post in Washington offer its services to law enforcement authorities "for the suppression of disorders and riots or anything threatening the constitutional form of government."

The Wobs and the Legionnaires, for all their polarity, were similar in many respects. Unfortunately, those similarities were all negative, particularly in Centralia. Both groups were populated by broad-shouldered men who either worked in the logging camps and mills or had fought in the war, or both. Young, sparsely educated, hard-driving, prone to reckless behavior, they were rough as the conditions that spawned them. There was no organ-

ization to which one could turn for moderation and prag-
matism in Centralia. The police, the politicians, even the
church had taken sides, all against the IWW. If the Wobblies felt persecuted and acted paranoid, perhaps they
were justified.

In September 1919, the IWW opened a union hall on
dingy Tower Avenue. It wasn't much, just a bare storefront on the ground floor of a beat-up rooming house.
But it gave them an aura of permanence and respectability that many in Centralia did not like. Everyone
remembered what had happened a year earlier, when the
first IWW hall in Centralia had been sacked by pipe-
wielding thugs. After setting fire to the hall, the raiders
beat up the Wobblies inside, threw them into a truck, and
drove them out of town, where they were dumped into a
ditch, beaten again, and warned never to return.

The Wobblies, always stubborn, came back anyway
and vowed among themselves to defend their new hall
from all attackers. Just as earnestly, a group calling itself
the Citizens Protective League—made up of local businessmen, civic leaders, and American Legion officials—
vowed to destroy it and drive the IWW out of Centralia
for good.

The two sides were put on a collision course on Tuesday, November 11, 1919, the date of the Centralia Armistice
Day parade, marking the first anniversary of the end of
the war. It was already seen as a flash point for Wobbly-
Legionnaire violence, and conflict became a near certainty
when it was announced that the parade would pass
through the center of town and then up Tower Avenue,
past the IWW hall—an odd route, considering that Tower

Avenue was the skid row of Centralia, lined with third-rate hotels, blistered old stores, pool halls, and soup kitchens.

The Wobblies thought they understood why their seedy neighborhood was being graced with the parade. There would be a "sting in the tail," they reasoned, a group of armed raiders who would drop out and attack the IWW hall after the rest of the marchers had passed.

Armistice Day was raw and gloomy in Centralia. This cut down the number of spectators considerably, which, as it turned out, was a good thing. After traversing the main streets, the parade turned up Tower Avenue and passed the IWW hall, led by the Centralia Legion Post in full army uniform. To the surprise of the Wobblies watching from within, the line of march didn't end with a "sting" but with a troop of Boy Scouts and several carloads of pretty Red Cross volunteers, waving and smiling. The Wobs were baffled.

Then an order to halt rang out, followed by an "about face!" The marchers turned on their heels and suddenly the parade order was reversed. The marchers again passed the IWW hall, now with the nurses and Boy Scouts in the lead, and the Legionnaires at the end. The sting was in place.

As the ex-servicemen reached a point squarely in front of the IWW headquarters, they abruptly began marching in place. Depending on whose account one reads, this was either an innocent action to close up the ranks or a deliberate prelude to pillage. Whatever its origins, someone suddenly cried, "Come on, boys! Let's get 'em!" and several hundred Legionnaires instantly broke formation and rushed the hall.

If the Wobblies were surprised at the parade's original order of march, the Legionnaires must have been shocked at what they found when they kicked down the hall's sagging door. Inside were seven men, one of them Wesley Everest. They were armed and there's little doubt they intended to shoot to kill. In a 16-by-35-foot room nearly every shot was bound to hit someone.

Amazingly, only three Legionnaires died in the hail of bullets that greeted them. But it was a brief fusillade; the defenders were quickly overwhelmed by the sheer number of attackers. Six of the IWW men retreated to an unused meat locker while the mob destroyed the hall and its contents. These Wobblies were later dragged out, beaten, and thrown into the Centralia jail.

Only one IWW man escaped: Wesley Everest. This undistinguished man suddenly became the pivot upon which years of mutual hatred turned.

Everest did not fit the Legion's portrayal of Wobblies as foreign agitators and traitors. He was a full-blooded descendant of Washington State pioneer stock and an army veteran who had served in France during World War I. But he was also a Wobbly, and now he was a revolutionist with his back to the wall. The military had taught Everest how to use a gun and he had, emptying his rifle into his fellow ex-servicemen as they stormed the IWW hall.

While his fellow Wobs were running for the meat locker, Everest grabbed his .45 Colt pistol and a pocketful of ammunition and escaped through a rear door of the building. Because he was wearing his army tunic he was momentarily mistaken for one of the attackers. It wasn't until he scrambled over a board fence that the crowd suddenly realized he was a Wobbly. They surged in pursuit, knocking the fence to the ground with their weight.

A mad chase of a mile and a half ensued through the streets of Centralia, Everest not far ahead of the bellowing mob, each side firing wildly at the other, neither hitting anyone. The running fight led to the Skookumchuck River, which Everest first attempted to wade, then changed his mind and turned back to shore. There he stood, dripping and hatless, the river at his back, when his pursuers arrived.

Everest offered to surrender to the law. "Stand back," he called. "If any of you are bulls [police], I'll let you arrest me; otherwise lay off."

The mob answered by rushing him. Everest tried to fire from the hip, but his waterlogged pistol jammed. The crowd, fearing the gun, fell back while Everest reset the magazine, then raised the .45 with both hands and took deliberate aim. One Legionnaire continued to advance: Dale Hubbard, nephew of one of the leaders of the Citizens Protective League and the son of one of the men—a banker—who had plundered the IWW hall in 1918. As he charged, Everest pulled the trigger and shot twice. Hubbard paused—probably as startled as Everest that the gun had fired—then resumed his rush. Everest fired twice more and Hubbard dropped at his feet, mortally wounded.

Everest threw his empty pistol into the river and the mob was on him. He was kicked and pummeled, his face beaten to a bloody pulp, his teeth smashed out by a rifle barrel rammed into his mouth. A belt was wrapped around his neck and a rope was thrown over a telephone pole. "You haven't got the guts to hang a man in broad daylight," Everest growled at his tormentors, an observation that would prove prophetic. He was then dragged to the jail, where his battered body was thrown into a corridor. He lay there, bleeding and moaning, while his fellow IWW defenders, locked in cells on either side, looked on helplessly.

Mars rose over Centralia as night fell. An angry mob had been gathering outside the jail all afternoon and into the evening, cursing, blowing auto horns, flashing lights, throwing missiles through the windows, pointing loaded guns through the bars. The idea that the men inside had been defending rights guaranteed them by the Constitution apparently never crossed the minds of the crowd.

At 7 P.M. someone pulled a main switch in the power distribution building adjacent to the jail. Centralia was plunged into darkness. At that moment, vigilantes kicked out a panel in the jail's wooden front door and reached in to turn the key. Everest was half-carried, half-dragged outside and tossed into the backseat of one of several cars that were parked at the curb. The mob—estimated by reporters the next day at two thousand—shouted "Lynch him!" The cars disappeared into the night. The lights of the city came back on.

The death caravan drove to the wooden bridge over the Chehalis River at the western edge of town. From his position on the floor of one of the cars Everest lashed out futilely at his assailants. The Legionnaires of Centralia later claimed that at this point they castrated Everest, screaming, with a razor blade, but whether this was true or just braggadocio has never been confirmed.

While two of the cars blocked the bridge, Everest was dragged from a third car, squirming between the men who held him. In silence they threw a rope over one of the bridge's crossbeams. The other end, already tied in a noose, was slipped around Everest's neck. The men dropped Everest over the edge of the bridge, but he somehow managed to grab the planking with his fingers and held on. One of the Legionnaires moved forward and stamped on Everest's hand until his fingers broke. The young logger dropped to the end of his rope with an audible thud. For a while, with car lights illuminating the scene, the lynch party amused themselves by firing bullets into the swaying body. Then the mob returned to their cars and quietly drove away.

Early the next morning someone cut the rope and Everest's body fell into the river, where it floated in the shallows for several hours. Fearful that friends of Everest might rescue the corpse, a posse recovered it in the early afternoon. The bloated, mutilated body was taken to the jail and dumped back into the central corridor, where the Wobblies in their cells could see it, the noose still buried in Everest's neck. It lay there, rotting, for three days.*

Finally, on the night of November 15, a squad of armed deputies drove four of the imprisoned Wobblies to a field on the outskirts of town. The prisoners were forced to dig an unmarked grave in the dark and throw Everest's putrefying body into it. The authorities later

---

*It was probably at this point that one of the jailed Wobblies, nineteen-year-old Loren Roberts, lost his mind. He was spared the trial and prison sentences suffered by the others but spent the rest of his life in an asylum.

claimed this was necessary to prevent the IWW from taking pictures of the corpse.

The Wobblies got no sympathy from the local press. The editorial page of the *Portland Oregonian* damned the IWW's defense of their hall as "treason" and added, in its best purple prose, "It spits in the face of every mother who gave her son that democracy might be safe." The Legionnaires had only been "exercising the right of free assemblage for purposes undeniably worthy and noble," while the lynching was "the rough and ready justice of the old-time Vigilance Committee." Under the headline KICK OUT THE TRAITORS the *Tacoma News-Tribune* praised the Legionnaries as "loyal and faithful citizens" and noted that they were part of "the great army of boys in khaki who fought nobly and heroically to stay the hordes of the kaiser in France." Wesley Everest had been part of that same great army, but that was not mentioned by the *News-Tribune*.

Seven Wobblies were later convicted of second-degree murder in the Centralia Massacre, as the Legionnaires now called it, and were sent to prison for terms ranging from twenty-five to forty years, despite the jury's recommendation for clemency. The verdict was tainted by intimidation: the American Legion paid four dollars a day to any Legionnaire who would sit, in uniform, in the front seats of the courtroom; fifty came every day. Some even sat inside the railing in the space reserved for the principals. Meanwhile, the prosecution had arranged for a company of regular army soldiers to pitch their tents on the courthouse lawn and drill within earshot of the jury.

No one spent as much as a day in prison for the murder of Wesley Everest. There was never even an official inquest into his death. His killers were known in Centralia but no one ever attempted to identify them publicly, and those in office refused to prosecute them.

The Centralia Massacre was the final flareout of the IWW. Everest's portrait had a place of honor in Wobbly halls alongside those of Hagglund and Little, but his posthumous glory was brief. Within five years of his death, the IWW was a shell of its former self, weakened beyond recovery. Mass arrests and deportations of Wobblies—part of a nationwide paranoia known as the "Red Scare" whipped up by Attorney General (and presidential hopeful) Alexander Mitchell Palmer—cut the heart out of the union. Then the booming economy of the 1920s silenced the laboring class. "Revolt!" said the IWW. "Throw off your chains!" But the loggers and mill hands didn't want a revolution. They wanted workmen's insurance and mattresses on their camp bunks, and once they got them they lost their will to fight.

The Legionnaires of Centralia commissioned a bronze statue to honor their fallen comrades. It still stands today, in City Park, its inscription describing the Legionnaires as "Slain on the streets of Centralia, Washington, while on peaceful parade wearing the uniform of the country they loyally and faithfully served." For many years Centralia schoolchildren were herded to the statue on Armistice and Memorial Days.

There is no corresponding monument for Wesley Everest, who according to his standards also served his country loyally and faithfully. It wasn't until the 1990s that a small plaque appeared just west of the Legionnaire statue, acknowledging "the coming of change" and recognizing the role of unions in establishing Social Security and the eight-hour work day. Although the plaque has a hangman's noose engraved on it, it makes no mention of Wesley Everest or the IWW. They are still sensitive subjects in Centralia.

# 19

# The Oilman Cometh

In 1857 James Townsend was in trouble. He was the president of the City Bank of New Haven, Connecticut, and the principal investor in a fledgling company called Seneca Oil. It was a bad company, nothing more than a stock promotion scheme run by a couple of third-rate New York lawyers who had little business experience and even less ethics. Yet Townsend believed that the venture was based on a sound idea: that underneath the banks of Oil Creek, near the obscure backwoods town of Titusville, Pennsylvania, lay a vast reservoir of what was then known as "rock oil."

Chemists who had tested this oil assured Townsend that it would make an excellent fuel for lighting and a superior industrial lubricant. It would sell, they said, for $20 a barrel, and the demand would outstrip the supply. If the company could get it out of the ground cheaply and quickly, its backers—Townsend chief among them—would be rich.

Seneca Oil had leased a hundred acres of bottomland along Oil Creek, but no one was buying the stock. Without investors, the company couldn't afford to dig for oil, and without digging, no one would invest in the company. James Townsend was in a bind. If the company failed—which seemed likely—and if it was discovered that Townsend had been financially associated with it, his business reputation would be seriously tarnished.

Townsend was mulling over these problems when by chance he struck up a conversation with Edwin Laurentine Drake, who occupied a room in the same hotel as Townsend. Drake had been raised on a New York farm, was poorly educated, only partially literate, and a jack-of-all-trades by necessity. But Townsend saw something in the solemn, stolid man that he liked, and he told him his sad story of the company, the fortune that could be gained from the oil, and the shortsighted investors. Seneca Oil would fail, Townsend told Drake, unless it could find someone to take charge of its field operations, someone who was tenacious, and, most important of all, someone who would work cheap.

The tale Townsend spun must have sounded heaven-sent to the unemployed Drake, who had recently been dismissed from his job as a railroad conductor because of his chronic bad back. Drake was no visionary, but he recognized an opportunity when it dropped into his lap. He pressed Townsend to tell him as much as possible about the venture.

Townsend sized him up. Drake was frail and sickly and had no skills as a prospector, but neither did anyone else at Seneca Oil. He still had his conductor's pass, which meant he could travel to and from Titusville for

free. For the nearly insolvent company, that was significant. Townsend also realized that Drake was the exact
opposite of the scalawags who ran Seneca Oil. The company's shoddy business practices gave it a bad reputation
among potential stockholders, and Townsend knew that
if he was ever going to make money, he would need a
front man clean, serious, and trustworthy to put a good
face on what had until now been a bad investment.

As the majority stockholder of Seneca Oil, Townsend
had the final say in the company's financial decisions. He
hired Edwin Drake as General Agent of Seneca Oil at a
salary of $83 a month and ordered him to go to Titusville
and get the oil out of the ground as quickly and cheaply
as possible. How he did it was up to him. Townsend,
always on the alert for possible money-making opportunities, also offered to sell Drake stock in the company. The
nearly broke Drake not only took the bait, he turned over
his entire bank balance of $200. As Drake later lamented,
"My friend pulled me in, in trying to get himself out."

In a final gesture, Townsend christened his new
General Agent "Colonel" Drake. It was a pure fabrication
Townsend created to give Drake "prestige with the back-
woodsmen" and because it might help Drake establish
some credit, which the weakly financed Seneca Oil Company could certainly use. Drake hated the phony title, but he
was in no position to complain. To his dismay, it not only
worked as Townsend had hoped, but it stuck with him long
after he had left Titusville, the oil business, and the earth.

To understand the obstacles that Drake faced, it helps to
understand the state of the oil industry in 1858, the year
that he arrived in Titusville. It was nonexistent.

The only "oils" that most people knew about were vegetable oils and animal fats. Most of the world's population used candles for illumination. Industrial machinery was greased with lard. A cheap, plentiful fuel for lighting and lubrication was desperately needed, but the oil that came out of the ground was ignored. In fact, it was regarded as nothing more than a curiosity, bottled and sold as a patent medicine to cure toothaches and to purge intestinal worms.

The big problem with rock oil was that there wasn't much of it around. To get it, prospectors either dug shallow "seeping" pits or skimmed it off of the surface of streams and springs. Using these techniques, unchanged over thousands of years, six gallons a day at best could be gathered. The oil derrick did not yet exist; the only people using derricks in 1858 were miners searching for underground salt water, which many believed was runoff from the biblical flood of Noah. The notion that oceans of oil might also be found under the earth was considered preposterous.

In the beginning Drake did what other prospectors had done: he hired men with picks and shovels to dig a pit in the ground. The residents of Titusville rolled their eyes; they had tried the same thing and failed—as did Drake. But Drake only used his pit to gather a couple of barrels of oil that the company could show to potential investors back East. Once Drake had shipped the barrels, he turned to Plan B.

George Bissell, one of the company's owners, had suggested that oil might be pumped out of the ground like salt water. It was a crazy idea, based on the assumption that "veins" of liquid oil lay underground like veins of coal. Anyone who knew anything about geology scoffed at the theory. Drake, happily, was not a geologist. He liked Bissell's idea. He also knew that he had only a short amount of time before Townsend's patience and cash ran out. Oil seeping into hand-dug pits wouldn't meet his production quota.

Drake made up his mind to drill within minutes of visiting the Titusville property. Ignoring the protests of Seneca Oil's stockholders, he used Townsend's money to build a derrick, buy a boat engine and steam boiler to power his drill, and hire a salt-boring veteran, "Uncle Billy" Smith, to drill the hole. Every day afterward, Drake would ride the two miles from Titusville to the drilling site to supervise the work. Although his bad back tortured him, "Colonel" Drake was careful to maintain his aura of respectability by always wearing a stovepipe hat and frock coat.

Drake guessed that his well would have to go down a thousand feet to strike oil, but the chances of it ever reaching that depth remained remote at best. Problems arose almost immediately. The drill went down easy enough, but once it was removed the hole would fill with water and then collapse. Smith was stymied; they would never reach bedrock and the hoped-for oil at this rate. Then Drake had a brainstorm. Why not drive a pipe into the earth until it hit bedrock, then operate the drill inside the shaft? It was a simple solution, and it worked perfectly. Had Drake patented it, he would have died a wealthy man, for the technique has been used by well-drillers ever since. Drake, however, was focused on the immediate task before him, and he let the opportunity pass. That made him an excellent and dependable general agent for Seneca Oil, but a big loser in the long run.

By now over a year had passed since Drake had been given his title and his start-up money. Townsend's patience was at an end. He had always been leery of putting too much cash into what he considered a high-risk venture; now he refused to send any more. The directors of Seneca Oil, unable to sell any more stock, were equally unresponsive to Drake's pleas. But Drake would not give up. He kept the operation going with money out of his own pocket. More important, the people of Titusville, mostly farmers and lumbermen, had become curious about Drake and his faith in mechanical solutions. He had been fair, honest, and hard-working, and they tried to help him when they could. They gave Drake food, loaned him transportation, even fronted the money he needed to buy the pipe shaft for his well. Without their assistance, Drake would have failed. As it turned out, their generosity was repaid a millionfold and more.

Sunday, August 28, 1859, was a day of rest. The drill had reached 70 feet the previous evening—only another 930 to go before it reached oil, by Drake's calculations. There was no way it would ever reach that depth before the money ran out, no matter how generous the townspeople might be. Still, Drake, single-minded and calm as always, had insisted that the work continue. He was committed to drilling for as long as possible and would spend every penny he had to do it.

Smith, who lived at the drilling site, peered into the well hole this Sunday morning and saw a depressing sight; water had pushed its way to within ten feet of the surface. Sixty feet of water would have to be bailed out of the hole. Smith cursed, fashioned a dipper out of a piece of rain gutter, attached it to a length of rope, dropped it into the hole—and hauled out a pailful of crude oil. Startled, Smith poured it out, tried it again and again, but it was always oil, not water, that filled his tin dipper. The hole was filled with oil, and more was pushing up from below every second. Smith ran into town to tell Drake, and by the end of the day the two men had pumped twenty barrels of oil out of the seemingly bottomless well—280 times more than had ever been gathered in a single day in history. There was no dramatic gusher or explosion, just oil oozing to surface under its own pressure, steadily making its owners rich.

Word traveled like lightning about the "black gold" discovered in Pennsylvania. Titusville quickly became a boomtown, dubbed "Oildorado." Fortune hunters from the four corners of the earth began arriving within days of Drake's discovery in a mad scramble to buy or lease parcels of land along Oil Creek. Locals who kept their property drilled their own "kick-down" wells using their legs for power. The population of Titusville swelled from several hundred to fifteen thousand; the bottomlands along Oil Creek echoed with the sounds of a thousand drill bits chewing into the earth. Land values shot through the roof, farmers sold their produce for unheard-of prices, blacksmiths rented their teams and wagons for more cash in a day than they normally made in a year, merchants sold out their stock repeatedly no matter how much they charged, barrel makers became wealthy manufacturing a commodity that was often more valuable than the oil pumped into it. Fortunes were made overnight in Titusville. In fact, nearly everyone in town made money except Edwin Drake.

Tenacious and taciturn, Drake did not seem to grasp the importance of what he had accomplished. He refused to join the frenzy to buy or lease neighboring lands, believing that his well sat on "*the* vein," as he put it, and that all of the wells along Oil Creek—including his own—would quickly run dry. Besides, he would argue, his job was to manage the property of Seneca Oil, not to run off and try to make his own fortune at the expense of those who were paying him a salary.

The owners of Seneca Oil rewarded Drake for his loyalty by firing him only seven months after his strike. Disgusted and humiliated, Drake sold his stock for a pittance (to the delight of the rapacious oil men) and took a job as a Titusville justice of the peace, where he notarized the leases of those who continued to drill and grow wealthy. Jonathan Watson, who owned the property on which Drake drilled his well, earned $3 million before he retired. Charles Hyde, a local storekeeper, made $1.5 million from a single well. Still, Drake was calm and self-assured. Never mind the overnight millionaires, he told his worried friends, a steady income would prove a better investment in the long run. His aching back continued to plague him, leaving him weak from pain and discomfort, but he rarely missed a day of work.

After four years Drake took stock of his savings and found that he had only $6,000. This was considerably better than the $200 he'd had in the bank when he first met James Townsend, but it was still a humiliatingly small sum for someone in his position, and Drake was a proud man. After all, his discovery had helped to prop up the Union treasury during the Civil War and had made others rich. When a Wall Street firm offered him a job as an oil broker he jumped at the chance, sold his house, and left Titusville for good. He never realized that the New Yorkers only wanted the prestige of his name. When oil prices collapsed in 1866, Drake was cut loose without dignity, his money gone.

Ten years after Drake's strike, a Titusville man named Zeb Martin ran into Drake by accident in New York. The tall, immaculately attired "colonel" of 1859 was barely recognizable now, bent nearly in half from the pain in his twisted back, his clothes shabby, his face lined with misery. Drake had come to New York, he told Martin, to try to find work for his twelve-year-old son. The Drake family was penniless, living rent-free in a tiny cottage on the New Jersey shore. They survived by selling Mrs. Drake's needlework. The boy was their only hope of steady income.

Shocked by Drake's plight, Martin returned to Titusville—which by now had banks, bordellos, and an opera house—and tried to raise money to ease Drake's woes. Most of the oil men refused to contribute. Why should they give money, they argued, to a man who couldn't earn a living for his family? Still, Martin was persistent, and he managed to raise $4,800. It was a pittance, but the grateful Drake lived off of this for the next four weary years.

By 1873 Drake's health had failed completely and he was confined to a wheelchair. His tortured spine gnawed steadily at his strength. "If you have any of the milk of human kindness left in your bosom for me or my family," he appealed, "send me some money." Again the oil men were approached and again they were dismissive, including John D. Rockefeller, well on his way to controlling the nation's oil business and becoming America's first billionaire. The legislature of Pennsylvania, however, felt some measure of shame and passed a bill granting Drake an annuity of $1,500. It was an embarrassingly stingy pension when one considers how much Pennsylvania had profited from Drake's discovery, but it was all that Drake was to get. He spent the last years of his life sickly and wracked with pain, morose and reticent, and died in 1880 at the age of sixty-one.

No one from the oil industry attended his funeral.

Big Oil grew into a multinational octopus over the following two decades, fueling revolutions in industry, transportation, and even home cooking. Oil lamps gave people the freedom to read and to work after dark, oil furnaces provided heat where coal and wood could not, oil-powered engines drove machinery unimaginable in Edwin Drake's day. Yet Drake, the man who had made it all possible, remained forgotten.

Then in 1904 Henry Rogers, a vice president of Standard Oil Company, the monopoly founded by Rockefeller, had Drake dug up from his grave in Bethlehem, Pennsylvania, encased in a handsome bronze casket, and shipped back to Titusville, where he was reburied under an elaborate monument at the entrance to Woodlawn Cemetery. Its focal point was a bronze sculpture, *The Driller,* a mallet-wielding, muscle-rippled Adonis bearing absolutely no resemblance to the man it supposedly honored.

Drake's monument cost $100,000. The stonemasons who built it made more money from the oil industry than Drake ever did. Along with the Homeric platitudes chiseled into the marble tombstone, the sham title "Colonel" was added to Drake's name, perpetuating his embarrassment.

Of course the purpose behind the new tomb wasn't to please Drake. It was to soothe the troubled conscience of a Standard Oil vice president; to imbue oil executives—in imperishable marble—with qualities of compassion and respect; to fool future generations into believing that the oil industry had honored its founder in his own lifetime. Looking upon Drake's grave today, who would suspect that he died impoverished and ignored by the millionaires he had created, or that he had lain in an obscure churchyard for twenty-four years?

When Mrs. Drake died in 1919, she was laid to rest beside the body of her husband. No one from the oil industry attended her funeral either.

# Genius in Irons

ARTISTS ARE SOMETIMES SEEN AS PRISONERS, EITHER OF A demanding public, economic necessity, or themselves. Those who pity the figuratively bound might reserve some extra empathy for Thomas Greene Wiggins, arguably the greatest musical talent of the nineteenth century, and doubtless the most misrepresented and neglected of the twentieth.

Tom Wiggins was born in May 1849. Before the age of four he displayed a remarkable aptitude for music; by eight he was performing before capacity crowds; by ten he was being compared to Mozart and Beethoven. His prodigious memory, astonishing keyboard skills, perfect pitch, and effortless execution were lionized in his time—yet today he has been forgotten, his compositions are absent from concert halls, and the few musicologists and historians who recall his name consider him a freak.

That's because Tom Wiggins was blind. And he was the child of Charity and Mingo Wiggins, plantation slaves in Harris County, Georgia.

Tom was the property of "General" James Bethune, a Columbus lawyer and the editor of the *Cornerstone,* said to be the first secessionist newspaper in the Peach State. Although Bethune was a scholar, well versed in science, literature, and languages, he believed in slavery. Black people, he felt, were incapable of learning and of responsible behavior. Many whites on both sides of the Mason and Dixon line felt the same way.

Tom was less than two years old when he first began accompanying his mother on her cooking chores in the Main House. Because he was blind, Tom was considered worthless. But he had an acute sense of hearing and a keen interest in everything that made sound—and the Bethunes were a musical family.

One day Tom reportedly crawled into the parlor while the Bethunes were eating dinner and picked out several tunes on the piano that he'd heard played by the General's daughters. The family was amazed. Tom, without benefit of sight or instruction, was playing as well as any adult, and he was only three years old. General Bethune told Tom's mother that "Tom has as much sense as a horse or a dog"—and he meant it as a compliment.

In plantation society, a slave with unusual talents brought status to its owners. The General decided that Tom was worth some time and effort, so the boy was put under the tutelage of Mary, the oldest Bethune daughter and the most accomplished family pianist. She taught Tom the fundamentals of musical composition, showed him how to improvise, and trained him in music theory and the nuances of technique. Tom was brought to operas, concerts, and recitals held in and around Columbus to expand his repertoire. His remarkable memory did the rest.

Tom became the "house pet" of the Bethune plantation, and when his abilities exceeded those of Mary (as they quickly did) the General employed instructors from the city to continue Tom's musical education. It was more coaching than teaching, as Tom usually only had to hear a composition once, no matter how complex, and he could reproduce it flawlessly.

This unusual devotion to a slave's musical education did not arise from a sense of kindness or generosity. The General recognized that this formerly worthless blind child was property that, once improved, could become a source of handsome revenue. "There was money in him," his mother later lamented. The other members of Tom's family were not "pets"; his brothers and sisters were treated like all the other Bethune slaves. So were Tom's parents, who suffered the further indignity of being gradually locked out of Tom's life.

By the time Tom was six he had become a prized possession of the Bethunes. He could play nearly a hundred compositions from memory—works by Bach, Beethoven, Chopin, Lizst, Mendelssohn, Mozart, Rossini, Verdi—an astonishing feat for someone so young. He could improvise on operatic airs from *La Traviata, Sonnambula,* and *La Fille du Regiment;* recite in Latin and Greek; and sing in German, French, and English. He had also composed several original works for the keyboard, such as *Water on the Moonlight* and *The Rainstorm.*

Blind Tom, as he came to be known, gave his first public performance in October 1857. He was an immediate sensation. A tour followed, winning accolades for the "sable muse" in every Georgia city in which he appeared. The *Athens Southern Watchman* hailed Tom's performance at the University of Georgia as "the most remarkable ever witnessed in Athens, one that would put to blush many a professor of music."

And yet... even at this early stage in his career the Bethunes had made a fateful decision not to credit Tom's abilities to training, hard work, and skill. Instead, he was billed as a "genius without benefit of instruction." This was fraud, although in a larger sense it was correct. Tom was taught only what was needed to improve his composition and performance skills. Although there were many schools for the blind that Tom could have attended, he was kept in confinement in the Bethune home. Music would be all he would ever know.

In 1858 General Bethune leased Tom for three years to Perry Oliver, a Savannah tobacco planter. Oliver paid Bethune $15,000 for the right to exhibit the boy slave and to keep whatever profits he could make. It turned out to be a good deal for Oliver, who toured hundreds of cities with Tom and netted an estimated $50,000 from the deal. The wishes and feelings of the nine-year-old prodigy and his parents, of course, were not considered.

Oliver viewed Tom as a circus act and decided to market him to sensation-seeking audiences. He broadened Tom's performances to include novelties: Tom played two different melodies simultaneously while singing a third, all in different musical keys; he stood, facing away from the piano, and played difficult compositions behind his back; he delivered orations mimicking the tone and delivery of noted statesmen; and he reproduced the sounds of nature, machines, and a variety of musical instruments using only the piano keyboard. The most popular part of the act was another Oliver innovation: local musicians were invited onstage to test Tom's remarkable memory by performing difficult piano compositions—preferably their own creations—that Tom could not have heard before. The blind boy, after only one listening, would walk to the keyboard and immediately reproduce the song. Audiences were astonished.

Oliver dressed the boy genius in shabby clothes and advertised him as a lunatic. Tom's concerts were advertised as "seances," and his creative and retentive skills were said to come from some "unusual and unexplained power," perhaps even a "satanic gift." It was the first step in the public dehumanization of Tom. Overflowing crowds followed the Blind Tom exhibitions wherever they went. Money poured in. Tom, who received none of it, was put on a merciless four-show-a-day schedule.

Tom's popularity was so great that he was invited to give a command performance for President James Buchanan at the White House. One Baltimore reviewer declared Tom's keyboard skills to be "greater than Mozart"; a reporter from the *Philadelphia North American* called him "the greatest pianist of the age." William Knabe, a piano manufacturer, was so impressed by Tom that he gave the boy an elaborately carved rosewood grand piano. Above its keyboard was a silver plate bearing the inscription: A TRIBUTE TO GENIUS.

A genius he may have been to the musical cognoscenti and to those who could see beyond the racial stereotypes of the day, but that image did not suit Perry

Oliver, General Bethune, and most of the people who came to the Blind Tom exhibitions. Tom had grown into a gawky, clumsy adolescent, with the added handicaps of being black, blind, socially isolated, and deliberately undereducated. On the concert stage, where decorum and ritual ruled, his deficiencies were all the more magnified. Journalists began salting their reports with references to Tom's "restlessness of body" and "blankness of features." Reviewers began to dismiss him as a "freak of nature," as if Tom were a six-toed cat or an albino crocodile. Self-styled experts drew a distinction between Tom's keyboard mastery and Tom himself, as if his hands somehow acted independently of his brain.

When Perry Oliver's contract expired in 1862, Tom was returned to the Bethunes. For the next three years Tom's talents were used by his master to raise money for the Confederacy; in other words, to assist in the continual enslavement of himself and his family.

A typical Blind Tom show was a musical smorgasbord crafted to please the greatest number of people. Tom would begin by performing several difficult classical pieces, then improvise variations and fantasies on popular ballads and operatic airs. He would sing sentimental songs in a rich baritone and recite poetry and prose (often his own compositions) in several languages. Then would come the demonstrations of Tom's skills of verbal and musical mimickery, and finally the "testing" by audience volunteers.

After ten years of rigorous instruction Tom's keyboard skills had grown polished, his execution clean. He had become a virtuoso, one of the best classic performers of his day. He had added the coronet, French horn, and flute to his stable of musical instruments, and he was now a published composer. Tom created one of his most popular pieces, *Battle of Manassas,* after hearing one of the General's brothers describe the fighting in that Civil War battle. Tom mulled over the sounds of the conflict—the rolling drums, blaring bugles, thundering hooves, rattling muskets, and booming cannons—and encapsulated it in an episodic, descriptive piece for the concert piano. He was fourteen years old.

Despite Tom's continuing musical triumphs, the rigorous testing of his talent and memory remained a part of the show, following him to adulthood and the grave, as if someone, somewhere, would finally prove that his abilities were merely a clever trick. Tom apparently enjoyed the challenge. He would stand with his back to the piano and call out whatever notes, chords, or dischords had been randomly played. He would sing any sequence of notes of the most challenging intervals, with perfect pitch, that were yelled from the audience. And of course he would effortlessly reproduce after only one listening whatever piano piece was played for him.

By May 1864 even the pro-secession General realized that a Confederate defeat was possible. To plan for the post-slavery world, the university-educated lawyer made a "legal" agreement with Tom's illiterate parents. Tom would be indentured to the General until his twenty-first birthday, thus ensuring that no matter who won the war, Tom would remain the General's property for the next six years. He would receive food, shelter, and musical instruction, as well as an allowance of $20 a month. His parents would receive $500 a year plus "a good home and sustenance," which meant that they could continue to live on the Bethune farm in their slave shack and eat slave food. The General agreed to keep only 98 percent of what was left after all of the Bethunes' administrative and management costs had been deducted.

Some simple arithmetic will show what a sweetheart deal this was for the Bethunes. Assuming that Tom netted $20,000 annually (a conservative estimate) from his concerts and from the sales of his sheet music, at the end of the year Tom would have $240, his parents would have $500, and both would split $400 (the promised two percent of the net) for a grand total of $1,140. The Bethunes would keep the other $18,860.

Tom's parents, of course, had no way of knowing that they were being fleeced. His father, without access to any legal counsel, ignorant of any standard of comparison, hopeless of any other offer, convinced that this was the only way that his slave son could be guaranteed anything, signed the contract the only way he knew how, with an X. Tom's mother protested years later, "They stole my boy from me." But by then it was much too late.


The end of the Civil War brought an end to slavery for most African Americans, but not for Blind Tom.

General Bethune, his financial affairs having collapsed with the Confederacy, now needed his ex-slave more than ever. Only three months after the war ended, the Bethunes launched a tour of Blind Tom exhibitions in the North. "Lunatic" Tom was accompanied by Professor W. P. Howard, a private music tutor from Atlanta. The Bethunes paid the professor travel expenses plus the unheard-of salary in that day of $200 a month—ten times what they were paying the star of the show.

Now a strapping sixteen-year-old, Tom's unrestrained facial expressions and bizarre bodily movements onstage were more pronounced than ever. Devoid of mental stimulation, mesmerized by beautiful music—the only source of beauty allowed in his life—Tom increasingly resembled a child as he grew older. The General was not about to aid in helping Tom to learn more socially acceptable behavior, since he had learned from Perry Oliver that Tom's oddness, properly marketed, could increase profits. One audience enjoyed Tom because of his talent—but another, less kind, was attracted because he was an "idiot." The General satisfied them both.

The classical music establishment fully accepted the notion of "idiot Tom." Even years after Tom's death, the few music references that mentioned Tom regarded him, at best, as a human parrot incapable of independent creative expression. Harold Schonberg in *The Great Pianists* (1953) dismissed him as "a successful promotional myth... exhibited as a musical prodigy." *The Encyclopedia of Music and Musicians* (1937) declared that Tom only impressed "non-musical people" and regarded it as "sufficiently remarkable" that "a blind and idiotic negro should have been able to play the piano at all." None acknowledged that Tom's achievements were the result of professional training—he studied with some of the best teachers in the United States and Europe—and considerable practice.

Tom's only chance to lead a normal existence came while he was being exhibited in Cincinnati, Ohio, in July 1865. It was there that the Bethunes were slapped with a writ of habeas corpus by Tabbs Gross, "the Barnum of the African race," who claimed that he, not the General, was Tom's rightful guardian. It was a flimsy piece of legal chicanery designed to gain custody of a valuable piece of property—Tom—and it led to a trial in which it became apparent that both the Bethunes and Gross were more concerned with Tom's money-making potential than his welfare. That did not stop the defense from arguing that the General deserved to retain possession of Tom because he had been a "benevolent master." Tom would experience "probable sufferings" and "unhappiness" if he were forced to leave the General's care, the defense explained, although they failed to mention that Tom had already spent three years away from the General under Perry Oliver with no apparent misgivings. The prosecution countered that the Bethunes had already made a fortune from Tom without any of that money benefiting him or his family, except through specialized education that only made Tom better able to make money that he would never receive. This could hardly be considered benevolent, but the judge did not see it that way.

The decisions handed down by Judge Woodruff of the probate court were perhaps typical of the mindset of the time, though they make remarkable reading today. He ruled that Tom was "mentally incompetent" despite the evidence of Tom's ability to learn and despite his published musical compositions and oratory works.*

---

*One of Tom's poems, titled simply "Blind Tom," ended this way:
*The perfume of the flowers that are hovering nigh—*
*And what are they—on what kind of wings do they fly?*
*The sun, moon and stars are to me undefined*
*Oh, tell me what light is—I'm blind, oh, I'm blind.*

Although the General admitted under oath that he would still "defend slavery as best for black people," the judge thought of him as a "good and humane slavemaster" and considered Tom's indenture agreement to be both legal and fair.

Tom's supposed mental incompetence was overlooked when Judge Woodruff ruled that Tom was "sufficiently able to choose his own guardian." The judge denied the prosecution's request that Tom receive a larger share of his concert proceeds; it would interfere with the "vested rights" that Tom's parents had agreed to when they had signed the General's contract. To the request that Tom receive an education that went beyond musical instruction, the judge replied that "forcing an education on Tom might weaken Tom's natural gifts" and denied him that, too.

Because of the rulings of Judge Woodruff, Tom became the chattel property of a man who had actively championed slavery and who was neither repentant nor reconciled. The General would continue to realize 98 percent of Tom's income, with no contractual guarantee that Tom or his parents would even see the 2 percent promised them. General Bethune was lauded as an example of moral rectitude as he dragged his quasi-slave out of town, thinking of new ways to make money from him.

It wasn't difficult. The publicity surrounding the trial was so great that Tom's performances at Philadelphia's Concert Hall—then considered America's foremost cultural center—were extended to four weeks from their original one. A group of the city's most esteemed musicians and scientists were invited to challenge the teenage prodigy with a battery of tests. They walked away as amazed as everyone else. "Under every form of musical examination," they concluded in their signed statement, "he showed a power and capacity ranking him among the most wonderful phenomena recorded in musical history."

Many theories were advanced to explain Tom's abilities, though few credited his diligent study and practice. All ignored the most obvious explanation: Thomas Wiggins had talent. A reporter from *New York World* thought that phrenology (analyzing the bumps on Wiggins's head) would unravel the mystery of the "black Beethoven." A spiritualist in Boston claimed that Tom's virtuosity came "from the other world where spirits were speaking through him." The *Philadelphia Inquirer* reported that, "according to some, Tom is an educated musician, painted Black, pretending to be blind, and with his hair curled in imitation of a negro's by a mode known to fashionable ladies."

The controversy made good copy and brought in the crowds, which is all that mattered to the Bethunes. Appearances in New York and Boston proved successful and lucrative, as did Tom's 1866 concert tour of Great Britain. He toured Europe in 1867, Canada in 1872, the Rocky Mountain states and the Far West in 1873, South America in 1875, then Europe again in 1880. Standing-room-only audiences were common. Tom relished the applause, but for all his travel he was more isolated than ever. His life consisted solely of concert halls, hotel rooms, and train rides between cities.

When Tom Wiggins turned twenty-one his indenture agreement with the General was at an end. It might have marked a happy turning point in his life, but there was no way that the Bethunes were going to let Tom get away. With a cautious eye toward any future legal challenges, the General had Tom declared insane and then had himself declared Tom's legal guardian. He transferred Tom's active management to his oldest son, John. The exhibitions continued as before, eight months out of every year, mid-October through mid-June. Tom's parents, who still lived on the Bethunes' Georgia plantation, were too poor to hire a lawyer to challenge the General for custody.

With the money he had raked in from fifteen years of Blind Tom exhibitions, the General bought a second farm on 420 acres of prime real estate outside Warrenton, Virginia. There, Tom was given a room with a piano in it and encouraged to practice continually whenever he wasn't touring. It was a minor inconvenience to the Bethune family, but it helped ensure that Tom would have as little interaction as possible with the world outside the concert stage.

In 1877 John Bethune and Tom began living in a boardinghouse in New York City during Tom's four-month summer hiatus, so that Tom could enlarge his repertoire and receive professional instruction to improve his technique. John eventually married the house owner, Eliza Stutzbach. Then, in 1884 he was run over by a train—and Eliza discovered that John had cut her out of his will in favor of his father. Eager for revenge, she swore she'd get her hands on Tom.

The following year Eliza employed Tom's aged mother in an attempt to wrest control of Tom from the Bethunes. Eliza claimed that Charity Wiggins, as the "nearest kin," was better qualified to custodial rights of her son than the General; unlike in 1865, neither side in this trial questioned that Tom was an idiot. As part of the deal, Tom's mother was moved to New York City and gave her word that Eliza would be appointed Tom's new guardian.

Helpless, confused, and now thirty-seven years old, Tom declared that he wanted to remain with the General. Tom's ex-slavemaster and principal exploiter was the closest thing to a friend that he had.

On August 16, 1887, over twenty-two years after the end of the Civil War, Tom Wiggins was finally removed from the custody of the Bethunes. His repertoire of classical music, all flawlessly memorized, contained nearly seven thousand works. He'd published more than a hundred compositions, from his early imitative pieces to later, more complex works such as *Wellenklänge* (a concert waltz) and *Rêve Charmant* (a piano nocturne). He'd given thousands of performances, visiting three continents and nearly every large American city. He had earned an estimated $750,000 for his ex-slaveholders. Yet Tom was handed over to his new guardians with nothing more than a trunk of clothes and his silver flute, valued at $175. The General was ordered to pay Tom $7,000 in back earnings, but the Bethunes claimed that the money had been swallowed by legal fees.

The *New York Times* reported that "now... whatever he will be able to earn above his expenses will inure to his own benefit," but it was not to be. Tom continued to perform throughout the United States and Canada until a few years before his death, but he was a source of income for Eliza Stutzbach, not himself. She promoted Tom as "the last slave set free by order of the Supreme Court of the United States!" but with the exception of his reunion with his mother, about whom Tom frankly did not care, nothing had changed.

Tom died of a stroke in Hoboken, New Jersey, in 1908, two weeks after his fifty-ninth birthday. With his parents dead, his siblings scattered, and the Bethunes no longer interested, only a handful of people attended his burial.

Like Chopin, Tom had composed a funeral march for the occasion, said to be a beautiful, haunting piece by those who'd heard it. But the organist at the Frank Chapel Undertaking Company was not familiar with Tom's work. The most publicized American pianist-instrumentalist-vocalist-orator-composer of the nineteenth century went to his grave to someone else's music.

# 21

# *Rugged Individualist*

ONE OF THE MOST ENDURING MYTHS IN AMERICA IS THAT of the rugged individualist, the lone man or woman with a good idea or noble cause who triumphs because our system of free enterprise recognizes and rewards such behavior. It stems from the days of the early pioneers, when independent-minded men and women were needed to wrest control of the Western Hemisphere from those who already lived here. The lure of forging one's own destiny was an effective way for European governments to put troublemakers to profitable use, and it was fun while it lasted, but the same rugged individualists who brought civilization to the wilderness quickly discovered that civilization, once established, had little tolerance for rugged individualists. Those who continued to act independently often found themselves in jail or dangling by the neck from a tree.

Edwin Howard Armstrong was a nobody from Yonkers, New York, who believed the myth. He showed promise at

Columbia University's School of Engineering and was fortunate in having a professor who gave him the time to pursue his inventions. It paid off generously, for Armstrong turned out to be a genius at electrical engineering. Working alone, sometimes in the attic of his parents' home, he invented the feedback circuit in 1912 and the superheterodyne in 1918, which brought wireless communication out of the Dark Ages of Morse code and into the living room of nearly every American.

The feedback circuit and the superheterodyne are not sexy populist products like the phonograph and the telephone. But without them radio and television would not exist, for they vastly increase the ability of wireless receivers to pull in and amplify signals. Armstrong—on a par with Bell, Edison, and the Wright brothers—was one of the great practical inventors of his time.

In the beginning, his faith in rugged individualism seemed justified. The ambitious men who were building empires in radio recognized that Armstrong's inventions would ensure their own advancement, and they rewarded him handsomely for his efforts. By the late 1920s—thanks in no small part to the feedback circuit and the superheterodyne—radio had become the most popular and profitable entertainment medium in history. Its executives, with the help of similar-minded men in Washington, formed a network oligopoly that made them rich. Armstrong was carried along on the general wave of prosperity. By the time he turned forty he was one of the largest single shareholders of RCA stock and a multimillionaire.

Most people in Armstrong's position would retire to a life of ease, speeches, and honorariums. But Edwin

Howard Armstrong was still an inventor and an individualist, albeit a wounded one, for in the early 1930s he lost a lengthy battle in the courts for the right to claim the feedback circuit as his own. The judges in the patent trial, ill equipped to understand the technical arguments involved, had ruled against Armstrong and in favor of Lee DeForest, a predatory inventor who had come along with a similar, inferior device. In their zeal to minimize Armstrong, DeForest's attorneys had gone so far as to suggest that Armstrong really wasn't an inventor at all. That got Armstrong's dander up. If the courts wouldn't recognize that he was worthy, he would prove it to them—and to the world—in the only way he knew how. He would invent something even more spectacular than the feedback circuit.

The most vexing problem facing radio in the 1930s was static, as anyone who has listened to an AM station during a thunderstorm will understand. Radio stations tried to filter it out or to override it by boosting transmission power, but the annoying crackling was embedded in the waves that carried AM. There was no way to separate the static from the music and voices. The engineers and scientists of the day shrugged their shoulders and called it hopeless.

Hopeless causes appealed to Armstrong's obstinate turn of mind. If AM radio was hopelessly flawed, why not invent a new kind of radio, one that wouldn't be affected by static?

It was radical—and dangerous—new territory for the former boy-wonder inventor, for if successful, it would turn the broadcasting industry on its head. Perhaps not surprisingly, that also appealed to Armstrong. He was well aware that the corporate giants that controlled radio and had been so accommodating of his independent ways when it had profited them had been unhelpful to him—and quietly cooperative to DeForest—in the feedback circuit patent trial.

To invent a new kind of radio, Armstrong first had to create an entirely new way of broadcasting. Then he had to invent new circuitry to produce it and new antennas, transmitters, and receivers to use it. The task was Herculean—it took Armstrong six years—and it would have been impossible for an individual, no matter how rugged, unless he was a genius and was rich. Happily, Armstrong was both.

In AM, sound is carried by varying the height—or "amplitude"—of the radio wave. So are the electrical disturbances that cause static. Armstrong decided to bypass this defect by keeping his radio waves at a constant height and instead varying the horizontal distance—or "frequency"—between them. Armstrong's radio would abandon amplitude modulation (AM) for frequency modulation (FM). It worked. In fact, it proved successful beyond Armstrong's wildest dreams. Not only was FM static free, it delivered audio of unimagined clarity and fidelity. When music was broadcast, it came through crisp and clear; when it stopped, the silence was velvety. With FM, even the most subtle and complex symphonic music could be sent over the airwaves with all of the rich overtones and naturalness that AM was unable to deliver.

Armstrong gave a private demonstration of FM to David Sarnoff, chairman of the board of RCA, in December

1933. Sarnoff was Armstrong's friend, a builder of empires who had publicly boasted on more than one occasion that obsolescence was the price of progress. This position suited him when, for example, RCA introduced Armstrong's superheterodyne, which so improved the home radio that the public had to buy new sets and make RCA more money.

Now Sarnoff and RCA were established, and AM was the cornerstone of their power. Obsolescence no longer seemed like such a good idea. If FM, which was so vastly superior in sound reproduction, was allowed to enter the market, then a new group of entrepreneurs would be able to provide a better product than the large networks. AM radio would be swept away, as would RCA's profits and Sarnoff's power.

Armstrong later recalled that Sarnoff remarked, "This is not an ordinary invention—this is a revolution," and promised his old friend that RCA would help develop FM. Flush with success, Armstrong failed to perceive Sarnoff's true feelings. It later became clear that the RCA chairman had already decided to crush Armstrong's invention.

At first, Sarnoff hoped that FM would simply fall flat when subjected to the rigors of RCA's broadcasting trials. But this was a vain hope, for the new radio system proved it could transmit farther and with greater clarity than any AM station. Radio engineers frankly couldn't believe it. The best AM stations had a signal-to-noise ratio of thirty to one; Armstrong's FM was a thousand to one. And Armstrong's small test transmitter broadcast over a wider area than all but the largest superpower AM stations in existence. The implications were staggering to network executives; once FM went on the air with full power, there would be no way to stop it.

When FM failed to fail, Sarnoff next tried to kill it by pretending that it didn't exist. RCA blanketed the press with advertisements and pages of copy promoting the network's newest venture, television, but made no mention of FM. Meanwhile, Armstrong was kept in limbo while RCA's engineers ordered more tests, more measurements, over and over again.

Armstrong was no neophyte, and when RCA kicked his FM broadcasts off of its experimental transmitter in 1935 he knew that Sarnoff—the most powerful man in the communications industry—was against him. Armstrong would have to shoulder the burden for bringing FM to the public alone.

Armstrong would also have to battle to get its basic concepts accepted. With the quiet backing of RCA and the big networks, a disinformation campaign was already under way to discredit FM and its inventor. FM, it was said, was an interesting technical achievement, but it was too wasteful of frequencies, too limited in range, too complex and expensive for receiver manufacture to ever be practical. It was also whispered that Armstrong was a "discredited inventor," a slippery allusion to his lost court case of ten years earlier. Most insulting of all was the claim that the public had a "tin ear" and didn't really want high fidelity in radio. Armstrong replied acidly that if this were true, special filters should be built in every concert hall to screen out those parts of the music that the audience didn't want to hear.

Most of this anti-FM claptrap was delivered by radio industry "experts" who were either connected by title or professional practice with the broadcasting corporations. Through these hatchet men, network executives could remain mum on the subject while at the same time FM was slowly talked to death.

Armstrong decided to show radio listeners what they were missing. He cashed in a block of his RCA stock and bought property atop some of the highest hills surrounding New York City. On top of one in Alpine, New Jersey, he erected a huge antenna and built the world's first FM radio station, W2XMN. In 1939 there were still only twenty-five FM radio sets capable of picking up its broadcasts, but high fidelity in radio had been proven. The clarity and resonance of Armstrong's signals blew away all arguments that had been raised against it. FM was reliable, its stations actually conserved frequency space by overlapping each other without interference, and it could cover greater distances than AM using the same amount of electricity. Most important of all, once people heard FM they loved it.

Unknown to Armstrong, RCA had been frantically developing its own FM system once it became apparent that Armstrong wasn't going away. Unable to destroy FM by attacking or ignoring it, RCA now wanted to minimize FM's impact by co-opting it.

Sarnoff sought the last refuge of the rich and powerful—he tried to buy Armstrong with a deal. In the fall of 1940 he personally offered Armstrong's attorneys a cash payment of $1 million. Sarnoff wanted three things for his money: all of FM's profits, all of its control, and the scientific credit for its invention.

In Sarnoff's fantasy world, Armstrong would license his FM patents to RCA free of all royalties. Armstrong would look the other way while RCA claimed that FM was the invention of RCA engineers. He would cooperate in putting FM on the air at low power and with cheap receivers, which not coincidentally would lessen its superiority to AM. And he would allow Sarnoff to mold FM into a network subsidiary, ensuring that it would never become a threat to RCA or to any other member of the communications elite.

Armstrong was livid. His goals were non-material and had nothing to do with maintaining the status quo. He wanted to be recognized as the sole inventor of FM. He wanted the best possible FM on the airwaves. And he wanted FM free and available to everyone, whether they wanted to operate a small local station or the biggest, most powerful radio network imaginable.

Armstrong flatly rejected Sarnoff's million-dollar offer, to the astonishment of RCA management. "What more does he want?" one dumbfounded executive asked, unable to fathom a man who valued principles more than money.

World War II brought a temporary halt to the FM battle, but it was clear that once it resumed it would be bloody. FM was winning more adherents every year. Mobile radios for police and public utility crews, a field once dominated by RCA, were now FM. The short-range communications systems used by the army and navy were FM. Even the audio signal used for television broadcasts—much to David Sarnoff's embarrassment—was FM. In fact, the only place still lacking FM was commercial radio.

In order to make this final push, FM needed frequencies on which to operate. The Federal Communications

Commission (FCC) was the government body that allocated those frequencies, and FM had only been given a very narrow band, sandwiched between AM and television, barely enough to hold forty channels. FM needed access to the shortwave frequencies above television if it was to have any chance to grow.

Unfortunately, the FCC in those days displayed a cozy loyalty to America's communications giants. Its position as a regulatory agency gave a veneer of respectability to rulings that flatly outlawed competition. Its chairmen had a history of spearheading decisions that were favorable to the business interests of Sarnoff and his friends, then afterward being hired for plum jobs with CBS, NBC, or RCA.

Over a thousand applications for FM station licenses were on file with the FCC by the spring of 1945. Well over five million FM radio sets were expected to be sold in the immediate postwar years. Nevertheless, despite the public's expressed support for FM and FM's track record of flawless performance, the FCC assigned FM frequencies far, far up in the ultra-shortwaves, and then it took away the frequency band that FM had been using since 1940. With one swing of the chairman's gavel, all of the radio stations that Armstrong had subsidized with his own money, and all of the half-million FM radio sets that had already been sold to eager listeners, were instantly useless. It was a crippling blow to a fledgling industry, engineered entirely in the interests of the big networks.

The FCC defended its decision by claiming that, despite FM's problem-free service, the lower frequencies were prone to interference from sunspots. Then the commissioners, without a hint of shame, handed those frequencies over to RCA television, which used FM for its audio.

The FCC wasn't through. It adopted a suggestion from CBS, called the Single Market Plan, that cut the transmitter power of every FM radio station to a fraction of its prewar level so that each could serve only a small geographic area. The plan was presented to the public as a way to open the airwaves to more FM stations, but that was a flimsy argument, since the ultra-high frequencies that had been given to FM had endless room for expansion. The real purpose of CBS's helpful suggestion was to crush any FM station powerful enough to act as the hub of a potential FM network. FM had been uprooted, hamstrung, and left to wither and die by the political clout of the communications industry.

Armstrong would not give up. He threw himself back into the fight with the grim intensity of a man obsessed, which by now he was. He had been counting on the swift postwar development of FM to replenish his treasury, but now he had to spend two more years funding research and building transmitters and receivers that would operate on FM's new frequencies. This he did without a second's thought, although those around him began to question whether the battle was really worth it. Armstrong thundered that "a crime has been committed against the radio art," and he would tolerate no compromise. After all, this was America, the land of opportunity. It was inconceivable to him that a scientific advancement that had been proven practical, that was far superior to anything in the marketplace, and that had the demonstrated support of the buying public could be crushed for

the benefit of a few self-serving men. Armstrong still
believed the myth.

By the end of 1949—thanks mostly to Armstrong's iron
will—over six hundred new FM stations were on the air.
The eagerness of music lovers for high-fidelity broadcasting remained strong. FM did not die.

It was, however, slowly being strangled by the noose
of regulations that had been wrapped around it by the
networks and the FCC. Armstrong, recognizing that his
emotional and financial resources could not last forever,
decided to confront RCA with a last-ditch legal attack, a
patent infringement suit that would, if successful, award
him triple damages on all FM and television equipment
that had ever been manufactured by RCA and its
licensees. It was a bold move—one man against the
power and money of some of the largest corporations on
earth.

RCA's lawyers turned Armstrong's litigation into an
ordeal of pretrial depositions and personal harassment
that dragged on for five years. The corporation's strategy
was simple: either FM, Armstrong, or Armstrong's bank
account would give out before the suit would ever reach a
courtroom. Cold and calculated as it may seem, it was
simply the position of a corporation defending its business. Lost somewhere in RCA's cost-benefit analysis,
however, was the understanding that their opponent was
not another multi-billion-dollar conglomerate but a
deeply wounded human being, driven by forces that
could not be tallied on an adding machine tape.

By early 1954 RCA's strategy had worked. Armstrong
was broken and at the end of his rope financially. He

realized that he had to accept RCA's buyout offer to survive, and he understood that once he did he would compromise both his hard-fought independence and the golden promise of free FM. It crushed him.

Armstrong's marriage lay in tatters as well. His wife of thirty years, whom he loved dearly, had begged him to end the suit on the best possible terms and leave the decision to history. When he refused, she walked out. His own suffering was tolerable, but he could not bear the thought that his battle for FM had caused her pain as well. He blamed himself.

On the night of January 31, 1954, Edwin Howard Armstrong put on his hat, overcoat, gloves, and scarf—and calmly walked out the thirteenth-floor window of his Manhattan apartment. A doorman found his body the next morning. The funeral was attended by David Sarnoff and other top RCA executives, but the true barometer of their feelings lay in the postmortem accolades given to Armstrong, the man who had made all broadcasting possible. There were none. AM radio ignored his passing entirely.

Less than two months after his death, Armstrong's beloved W2XMN went off the air for good. He had poured more than $2 million of his own money into its development. But FM's champion was dead, and no one was willing to take up his banner. The corporation had won.

It would fall to another generation, still in their infancy when Armstrong took his own life, to resurrect FM. In the late 1960s overseas manufacturers, free of America's AM radio tyranny, began exporting to the United States radios capable of receiving both AM and

FM, something we take for granted today. Independent broadcasters bought unprofitable FM stations and used them to play the musically complex rock music of the time. Youthful baby-boomers embraced FM's high fidelity as their classical-loving parents had in the 1940s, and advertising dollars followed. Thirty years later FM is the rightful broadcast champion for music and AM is principally a medium for talk, as it should have been in 1950.

A friend of Edwin Armstrong observed twenty-five years after the inventor's death, "Many good things happened for him, but too many happened after he had already killed himself."

# 22

# The Enemy Within

THE MORNING LIGHT SEEMED UNNATURALLY BRIGHT TO
Jerry Tarbot. A large hospital orderly in a white coat stood
over him, splitting the sunbeams as Jerry fought his way
into consciousness. He remembered that he had been
wounded.

"Is this a Frog joint?" he asked the orderly. "Any of
my outfit in the other room? What town are we near?"

To Jerry Tarbot the year was 1918 and he was in
France, behind the Allied lines, probably near the
Château-Thierry sector. But he was not there, or any-
where near it. In fact, he had awoken in the California
State Hospital for the Insane at Stockton. The year was
1923.

What had happened to Jerry in those intervening five
years was a mystery. Apparently shell-shocked and
amnesic, Jerry Tarbot was a sickly man with a scarred face,
a left cheek that had been grafted on, and lung damage

and limb infections indicative of poison gas. He also had an old, nasty bullet wound to the head. He was known as a "screamer" at Stockton because he would go mad with terror at loud noises. He seemed to be in his early thirties.

No one knew where he had come from or what his real name might have been. He'd gone by "Jerry Tarbot" when he'd been picked off the streets of San Francisco the previous year, chasing imaginary German soldiers with a bayonet tied to the end of a broom, but where that name came from no one could say, least of all Jerry. Nevertheless, the judge who signed his release papers in 1923 made it official. Jerry Tarbot would be his name, at least until someone could be found who knew his real one.

That would prove more difficult than anyone at that time could have imagined.

The story of the shattered doughboy with the missing memory intrigued everyone who heard it, and efforts were immediately made to reunite Jerry with his missing past. His fingerprints were checked against all known World War I veterans with similar-sounding names. The American Red Cross got involved, as did the Foreign Legion, the War Department, and the Marine Corps. A local congressman, Albert Carter, got wind of the story and immediately brought special legislation before the House of Representatives that would give Jerry the right to compensation, a pension, and hospital treatment as a veteran. This brought the Veterans Bureau into the mix. Soon a half-dozen Washington agencies had their employees tracking Jerry Tarbot's true identity.

Meanwhile, Jerry wandered up and down California, working odd jobs, entering charity hospitals when his body or brain broke down, gradually trying to recall his past. He believed he had served with the marines and had fought in the battles around Belleau Wood in 1918. His recollection of intricate details of the war front—nicknames of fellow soldiers, the topography of the region, specifics of troop movements—impressed every ex-serviceman who met him and convinced them that he had indeed seen hard service at the French front. He even met one man in San Diego, William Beach, who claimed to have been the Marine Corp medic who had grafted on his left cheek. But Beach could not recall Jerry's real name. Nor, for that matter, could anyone else.

In late 1925 a Los Angeles doctor hypnotized "the living unknown soldier" and watched as he dug trenches in the carpet and went over the top of the office furniture. He was also able to drag memories out of Jerry that hinted he had lived and worked in New York City before the war. Encouraged, Jerry enlisted the help of a Marine Corp general and worked his way east in the galley of a ship sailing from San Francisco. By the time he arrived in New York in early 1926 he was sick again and was packed off to a veterans hospital in Washington for a head operation.

While he lay on the operating table, he saw the tray of surgical instruments and suddenly remembered that he had worked at the J. Sklar Company in Brooklyn, which manufactured similar tools. Despite his fragile health, Jerry traveled to New York and was recognized by several of J. Sklar's employees as a man who had worked there between 1912 and 1914. But they couldn't remember his name, and the payroll records from that period had been destroyed. Similarly, several employees at the Brady Brass

Works in Jersey City remembered Jerry as a machine operator who had worked there in 1911. His name, however, eluded them.

Jerry's trip to New York opened the floodgates of his memory. He recalled that he had served mass as a boy at Fordham University for a Reverend O'Reilly. Fordham University was contacted; the Reverend O'Reilly had died in 1911. Jerry also recalled that he had worked in an antiques shop at the corner of Myrtle and Bedford Avenues in Brooklyn. The store was vacant when he visited, but a neighbor pointed out the house where the owner lived. Jerry walked to the house and found his former boss—stretched out on his burial bier. None of the man's family or friends could remember Jerry's name.

Details of Jerry's war service also began drifting back to him, but they weren't promising. Jerry remembered that he had tried to enlist, had been declared 4-F, and that "during my efforts to get into the Army some way, any way, I may have changed my name, fibbed about my nationality, my age." In the early spring of 1918, he recalled, he had shipped as a coal heaver on a freighter out of Boston to get to France, then reached the American sector and bluffed his way through for about a month.

"That was not difficult," he later wrote. "At that time, it was no trick to get a uniform. A few francs to a man who happened to be AWOL, a couple of bottles of cognac to a man detailed to the Quartermaster's Department, a surreptitious trip to the salvage heap.... Some of the men didn't like the war and dropped out of sight before they got to wherever they were supposed to go, leaving vacancies in the ranks. And nearly all the replacements were the dumbest things on God's green earth until they were broken in, so it was easy to be dumb and not answer questions. Once you had been assigned to a squad and given a number, you were in the Army, boy... if you showed any signs of life at all, there was nobody who had time to inquire about your pedigree. And if you could sling the Frog parley-voo, you stood ace high. I could talk some French."

If this were true, it meant that Jerry Tarbot, whoever he was, would have no fingerprints on file, no dog tags, no service record of any kind. If he had worn the uniform of another soldier, there would be no way to trace him once his mind had been blasted away by the German gas and shells. He could be listed as Killed In Action by the French, Belgians, Canadians, or Americans. Even the men he'd fought alongside might have known him by a name that was not his own.

Finding Jerry's true identity, it was rapidly becoming apparent, was a nearly impossible task. The organizations that had helped him (and received favorable press for their efforts) were growing weary. Jerry's demands were not exceptional—all he wanted was to find out who he was so he could receive veterans benefits—but Jerry was persistent. And the longer Jerry Tarbot remained in the spotlight, the more uncomfortable questions began to be raised about the military's sloppy handling of the war and Washington's often callous treatment of the men who had fought it. Jerry was no diplomat, and his strident criticism of "the deadening influence of charity hospitals" and "the sewer of chicanery surrounding the sick veteran" repeatedly bit the hand that fed him. It did not make Jerry friends with those who were giving out the goods.

Representative Royal Johnson was chairman of the House Committee on World War Veterans Legislation. He believed in the infallibility of military record keeping and in pulling one's self up by one's own bootstraps. He did not believe in traumatic amnesia or government-funded long-term medical care. He did not like Jerry Tarbot. In Johnson's opinion Jerry was the point man for a whole army of phony veteran "malingerers" lurking in the shadows, waiting to pilfer the public purse.

The House of Representatives had been unwilling to grant veteran status to Jerry until proof of his military service could be confirmed, and they had shunted that responsibility over to the Veterans Committee. Chairman Johnson, his mind already made up, ignored the dozens of ex-servicemen who swore that they had served with Tarbot—including a fellow congressman, Ralph Updike of Indiana, and Gene Tunney, the world heavyweight boxing champion—and instead called in agents of the Department of Justice. He ordered them to trace Jerry's history backward from 1923.

What they found was unsettling. Jerry's worst personal defect was not even a secret—he was occasionally insane. He'd been committed to the Stockton asylum in October 1922 because, in the opinion of the Superior Court, he was "dangerous to be at large" and "so far disordered in mind as to endanger health, property and person." Still, just because Jerry was crazy, that didn't make him dishonest.

But the Justice Department agents also discovered that prior to his commitment Jerry had been in jail, arrested for borrowing money against a car that was not fully paid for. It was a minor offense and the charges were dismissed, but the fact remained that "Jerry Tarbot," whoever he really was, had apparently been involved in some sort of scam. Chairman Johnson smelled blood and ordered the agents to keep digging. The information about the car was kept from the sympathetic public and even from Jerry himself, desperate as he was to uncover his past.

Years later, when Jerry was confronted with the agents' findings, he accepted them as entirely possible but incidental. He called the period before his awakening the "years of the brute" and regarded it as part of a previous life. "[I] never, never laid claim to have possessed a pair of wings nor a halo," he wrote in his autobiography. Regardless of what he had or hadn't done, there were still wide gaps in the record that allowed his World War I odyssey to have taken place, which was, after all, the supposed point of the investigation. He vehemently denied charges of any greater wrongdoing and felt that, whatever his previous indiscretions, he was still "entitled to be treated squarely."

Jerry, however, had run afoul of the chairman of one of Washington's most powerful congressional committees. A square deal from Royal Johnson would prove harder to find than Jerry Tarbot's real name.

While the Justice Department poked into his past, Jerry remained in New York, grateful to those who hired him for odd jobs, frequently appealing to the newspapers to print his photo and his story in the hope that someone would recognize him. Recognition he got; help he did not. A Manhattan elevator operator came forward and said that Jerry was really James Tarbet, manager of a private club in Havana who had abandoned his ailing wife and fled to Scotland. An ex-marine from Baltimore thought Jerry was George Beaupre, a French-Canadian who had been wounded in no-man's-land and subsequently vanished. A priest believed that Jerry was George Chapuis, a former prep school student at Fordham University. A Brooklyn man identified Jerry as Bruce Harpin, who had operated a lunch wagon in his neighborhood. All of these leads were followed; all led to dead ends. A Broadway producer invited "the mystery Marine" to appear onstage for a week and tell his story, but Jerry refused. "People would say the whole thing was just a publicity stunt," he explained, "just for the sake of getting on the stage." Merchants tried to hire Jerry for in-store appearances, but he declined those offers as well. "I had no use for the position of a decoy duck."

In October 1926 Jerry did go onstage, before thousands of veterans at an American Legion convention in Philadelphia. He stood under a spotlight, hoping that someone would recognize him. One man did—even recalling that Tarbot had served with the Sixteenth Company of the Fifth Marine Regiment—and verified that Jerry had indeed fought in the battle of Belleau Wood. Anxiously Jerry asked, "What's my name?"

The man stood silent for a moment. "I don't know," he finally replied. "If I ever did know I have forgotten it."

Further questioning led to more details but no identification. Jerry recalled that his commanding officer had been a Lieutenant Robinson. The man told him that Lieutenant Robinson had died later during the war.

More frustration came the following month when the *Times-Press* of Akron, Ohio, paid for Jerry to visit the

Goodyear Tire and Rubber plant, where he vaguely remembered being employed. The minute that he entered the plant a man rushed up and shook hands with him, shouting that the two had worked on the same gang. But he remembered Jerry only by his nickname, Buddy. In all, more than fifty people at the plant recognized him—none of whom could remember his name.

Goodyear put its clerical force at Jerry's disposal and together they went through the paybooks from November 1916 to May 1917, the period when it appeared most likely that he had been employed. None of the names meant anything to him. "My own name in front of my eyes," he recalled, "the name to which I had responded a thousand times . . . and it was wholly foreign to me."

In March 1927 Jerry was called to Washington to plead his case before the Veterans Committee. Events had reached the point of no return for Congress: not only was Representative Carter's bill before the House, Senator Edward Edwards of New Jersey had submitted similar legislation to the Senate, authorizing the Veterans Bureau to give Jerry the status of a disabled war veteran. Jerry had known for years that the Justice Department was probing into his background, and he figured that he'd be in for a grilling. What he got was more like an incinerator.

First, Chairman Johnson branded Tarbot a "slacker" and announced that he would prove that all of Jerry's claims were lies. "The committee members," he declared, "were going to force me to . . . put Tarbot on the government payroll for the rest of his life. I would not O.K. it because I knew Tarbot was a fraud, but I did not want to expose him unless I was forced to do it." Johnson then revealed Jerry's 1922 arrest and dramatically announced that Tarbot was actually Alexander "Frenchy" Dubois, son of a chef in a Cuban hotel. The Justice Department agents displayed handwriting samples, supposedly Dubois's, that resembled Jerry's.

"Do you have anything to say in your defense?" Johnson demanded. Jerry peered at the handwriting samples. "If you want to crucify me," he told the chairman, "go ahead."

Johnson trotted out Flora Dove Lange, who claimed that Jerry had married her in late 1917 and then had deserted her two weeks later. Under cross-examination, Lange admitted that she had been married four times and couldn't remember the name of the Justice of the Peace who had married her and Jerry. She also admitted that the parting had been mutual. Could she, one committee member asked, recall any identifying marks that would prove that the man she had married was Jerry? Yes, she replied, Jerry had an eagle tattooed on his arm. Jerry obligingly rolled up his shirt sleeves. There was no tattoo on either arm. Jerry stared at the attractive woman and laughed. "I might have married her," he said. "A guy is likely to go crazy once in a while."

For the next two days Jerry had to defend himself by reliving what he called the "mire of hell" of Belleau Wood. He pointed out that the Marine Corp colonel who had questioned him, at the committee's request, had concluded that "it is difficult for me to believe that Tarbot did not see hard service in France, or that he did not actually serve for a brief, but hectic, period with the Sixth Marines." He reminded Chairman Johnson that Dr. John J. Kindred, a congressman from New York and a physician specializing in mental disorders, had testified that Jerry was suffering from amnesia brought on by shell shock, and that the committee's own medical team had determined that Jerry was not a malingerer or a fake. He reasserted his claim to the legal status of a veteran, without documentary evidence, because he had been recognized by warfront veterans as a comrade-in-arms and because he bore the scars of combat on his body. He called the allegations against him "largely the fabrication of brains bent on defamation" and charged that Chairman Johnson was eager to discredit him because he was proof that not every person who served in World War I could be accounted for—a hot-button political issue in the 1920s.

Jerry Tarbot was going down fighting, but he had already lost the war.

What, exactly, had Chairman Johnson's investigations proved? If taken at face value—a big if—they showed that Jerry was an errant husband from a loveless marriage and that at one time he'd been involved in a penny-ante money-borrowing scam. Aside from that, the employment records gathered by Johnson's own investigators showed that "Frenchy" Dubois, the man they claimed Jerry was, had spent nearly all of his time gainfully employed as a machinist. The employment trail ended on February 2, 1918, leaving Jerry plenty of time to ship himself to France and participate in the May–June battles around Belleau Wood, as he'd always insisted he had. In short, even if Johnson's damning allegations were all true, they were irrelevant to whether or not Jerry had received debilitating wounds in battle.

But the public had grown tired of Jerry Tarbot. After years of work by the media and a number of well-intentioned organizations, no dramatic reunion with a family member or sweetheart had been forthcoming. That seemed suspicious. Jerry's tenuous grip on sanity did not help in winning friends either. Chairman Johnson sensed the uneasiness in the public mood, pointed out that there was no documentary evidence to support Tarbot's story, and then brought in the Justice Department to air its dirty laundry. That successfully shifted the focus of the hearings from Jerry's wartime service to Jerry's moral fitness. The hint of scandal cast a pall of disreputability over Jerry and his motherless doughboy image—an image that Jerry neither endorsed nor cultivated. But it was enough.

With a satisfied swing of his gavel Chairman Johnson postponed the Veterans Committee's action on Jerry Tarbot indefinitely, effectively denying him the status of a disabled war veteran. The popular press obligingly followed suit and dropped Jerry like a hot potato, as did the Red Cross, the Foreign Legion, and the Marine Corps. After 1927 the living unknown soldier virtually vanished from public view.

His fall from grace came so abruptly that Jerry Tarbot felt obligated to publish his own account of his life in 1928. It was the product of a disordered mind, difficult to follow at times, but in it Jerry made his case clear enough. "I am not a bigamist. I am not a crook. I am not a malingerer. I am not an imposter. Any man or woman who says that I am is a willful dirty liar!" It was also a voice crying in the wilderness. The book did not sell. Jerry Tarbot, so recently beloved by tearful mothers and ex-doughboys, was now more than unknown. He was persona non grata.

"Somewhere in France," Jerry Tarbot wrote, "there is a grave that bears the name of the man who was I. Under the cross that marks it are buried, probably, a few shreds of flesh and perhaps a piece of uniform, given my name because my comrades missed me and because the pitiful fragments needed a name. There it lies—the name I cannot pluck from behind the obstinate barrier."

Thwarted of his goal, Jerry Tarbot disappeared for good, an exasperating, pathetic figure. If he ever discovered who he really was, it went unreported. The living unknown soldier died in total obscurity.

# SELECT BIBLIOGRAPHY

I've shortened this bibliography to key sources that I felt would be most useful and accessible. For those who wish to investigate further, the *New York Times Index* (available in most major libraries) not only pinpoints contemporary *Times* articles about raw dealers, but helps narrow the search for articles in other publications. For recent written works you can use online searching, either through the Web or, preferably, a library periodicals database.

CHAPTER 1
Bradford, Phillips Verner, and Harvey Blume. *Ota: The Pygmy in the Zoo*. New York: St. Martin's Press, 1992.

CHAPTER 2
Weidenaar, Reynold. *Magic Music from the Telharmonium*. Metuchen, N.J.: Scarecrow Press, 1995.

CHAPTER 3
Lee, Martin A., and Bruce Shlain. *Acid Dreams*. New York: Grove Press, 1992.
Marks, John J. *The Search for the Manchurian Candidate*. New York: Times Books, 1979.
Thomas, Gordon. *Journey Into Madness*. New York: Bantam Books, 1989.

CHAPTER 4

Hoig, Stanley. *The Battle of Washita*. Garden City, N.Y.: Doubleday and Co., 1976.

———. *The Cheyenne*. New York: Chelsea House, 1989.

Wensteins, Irving. *Massacre at Sand Creek*. New York: Charles Scribner's Sons, 1963.


CHAPTER 5

Archer, W. Harry. "Chronological History of Horace Wells, Discoverer of Anesthesia." *The Bulletin of the History of Medicine* 7 (December 10, 1939).

Pernick, Martin S. *A Calculus of Suffering*. New York: Columbia University Press, 1985.

Taylor, Frances Long. *Crawford W. Long and the Discovery of Ether Anesthesia*. New York: Paul B. Hoeber, 1928.


CHAPTER 6

*Conserving Prairie Dog Ecosystems on the Northern Plains*. Bozeman, Mont.: Predator Project, 1996. P.O. Box 6733, Bozeman, MT 59771

Jacobs, Lynn. *Waste of the West*. Tucson, Ariz.: privately printed, 1991. P.O. Box 5784, Tucson, AZ 85703


CHAPTER 7

Advisory Committee on Human Radiation Experiments. *The Human Radiation Experiments: Final Report of the President's Advisory Committee on Human Radiation Experiments*. New York: Oxford University Press, 1996.


CHAPTER 8

Dana, Julian. *Sutter of California*. New York: Press of the Pioneers, 1934.

Dillon, Richard. *Fool's Gold: The Decline and Fall of Captain John Sutter of California*. New York: Coward-McCann, 1967.

Zollinger, James Peter. *Sutter: The Man and His Empire*. New York: Oxford University Press, 1939.

CHAPTER 9

Hortin, L. J. "Did He Invent Radio?" *Broadcasting Magazine* (March 19, 1951).

Horton, L. T. "Murray, Kentucky, Birthplace of Radio." *Kentucky Progress Magazine* (March 1930).

Morgan, Thomas Olin. "The Contribution of Nathan B. Stubblefield to the Invention of Wireless Voice Communication." Ph.D. diss., Florida State University, College of Arts and Sciences, 1971.


CHAPTER 10

Kohn, Howard. *Who Killed Karen Silkwood?* New York: Summit Press, 1981.

Rashke, Richard. *The Killing of Karen Silkwood.* New York: Penguin Books, 1982.


CHAPTER 11

Peskin, Allan. *Garfield.* Kent, Ohio: Kent State University Press, 1978.

Smith, Theodore Clarke. *The Life and Letters of James Abram Garfield.* New Haven: Archon Books, Yale University Press, 1968.

Taylor, John M. *Garfield of Ohio: The Available Man.* New York: W. W. Norton and Co., 1970.


CHAPTER 12

Lawrence, Joe, Jr., and Roger W. Brucker, *The Caves Beyond.* New York: Funk and Wagnalls, 1955.

Murray, Robert K., and Roger W. Brucker, *Trapped!* New York: G. P. Putnam's Sons, 1979.


CHAPTER 13

Beals, Carleton. *Brass-Knuckle Crusade.* New York: Hastings House, 1960.

Golden, Harry. *A Little Girl Is Dead.* Cleveland: World Publishing, 1965.

Woodward, C. Vann. *Tom Watson: Agrarian Rebel.* New York: Macmillan, 1938.

CHAPTER 14

Goodyear, Charles. *Gum-Elastic and Its Varieties*. New Haven: privately printed, 1853.

Wolf, Ralph F. *India Rubber Man*. Caldwell, Idaho: Caxton Printers, 1939.

CHAPTER 15

Wallace, Amy. *The Prodigy*. New York: E. P. Dutton, 1986.

CHAPTER 16

Mann, W. Edward. *Orgone, Reich and Eros*. New York: Simon and Schuster, 1973.

Mann, W. Edward, and Edward Hoffman. *The Man Who Dreamed of Tomorrow*. Los Angeles: J. P. Tarcher, 1980.

Reich, Ilse Ollendorff. *Wilhelm Reich: A Personal Biography*. New York: St. Martin's Press, 1969.

CHAPTER 17

Franklin, Robert J., and Pamela A. Bunte. *The Paiute*. New York: Chelsea House, 1990.

Morrison, Dorothy Nafus. *Chief Sarah*. Portland, Ore.: Oregon Historical Society Press, 1990.

Winnemucca, Sarah. *Life Among The Paiute: Their Wrongs and Claims*. New York: G. P. Putnam's Sons, 1883.

CHAPTER 18

Jensen, Vernon H. *Lumber and Labor*. New York: Farrar and Rinehart, 1945.

Miller, Joseph. *Solidarity Forever: An Oral History of the IWW*. Chicago: Lakeview Press, 1985.

Thompson, Fred. *The IWW: Its First Fifty Years*. Chicago: Industrial Workers of the World, 1955.

CHAPTER 19

Botsford, Harry. *The Valley of Oil*. New York: Hastings House, 1946.

Knowles, Ruth Sheldon. *The Greatest Gamblers*. New York: McGraw-Hill, 1959.

Yergin, Daniel. *The Prize*. New York: Simon and Schuster, 1991.

CHAPTER 20

Sifakis, Carl. *American Eccentrics*. New York: Facts on File, 1984.

Southall, Geneva Handy. *Blind Tom*. Minneapolis: Challenge Productions, 1983.

Southern, Eileen. *Biographical Dictionary of Afro-American and African Musicians*. Westport, Conn.: Greenwood Press, 1982.

CHAPTER 21

Bilby, Kenneth. *The General: David Sarnoff and the Rise of the Communications Industry*. New York: Harper and Row, 1986.

Erickson, Don H. *Armstrong's Fight for FM Broadcasting: One Man vs. Big Business and Bureaucracy*. Tuscaloosa, Ala.: University of Alabama Press, 1973.

Lessing, Lawrence. *Man of High Fidelity*. Philadelphia: J. P. Lippincott, 1956.

CHAPTER 22

Tarbot, Jerry. *Jerry Tarbot, The Living Unknown Solider: His Book*. New York: Tyler Publishing, 1928.

## About the Artist

Mack White's critically acclaimed comic book series, *Villa of the Mysteries*, is published by Fantagraphics. His work has also been featured in *Details*, *Gnosis*, *Heavy Metal*, and other magazines. He lives in Austin, Texas.

## About the Author

Ken Smith is a co-author of *Roadside America* and *The New Roadside America*. His last book, *Ken's Guide to the Bible*, left him with a stack of angry mail that he enjoys sharing with friends. He lives alone.